Lines from Lea Bailey

Lines from Lea Bailey

ROBERT CHOULERTON

THE CHOIR PRESS

Copyright © 2022 Robert Choulerton

All rights reserved. No part of this publication may be reproduced or transmitted in any form or by any means, electronic or mechanical including photocopying, recording or any information storage or retrieval system, without prior permission in writing from the publishers.

The right of Robert Choulerton to be identified as the author of this work has been asserted by him in accordance with the Copyright, Designs and Patents Act 1988

First published in the United Kingdom in 2022 by
The Choir Press

ISBN Paperback 978-1-78963-271-2
ISBN Hardback 978-1-78963-272-9

For James and Elizabeth

Contents

1	APPEAL	1
2	SUBJECTIVITY	3
3	CROW	5
4	WORC	7
5	NURSERY RHYME	10
6	SOU' WESTERLY	11
7	THE ENGLISH WAY	12
8	VOLUNTEERS	14
9	ANTHEM FOR ENGLAND	16
10	INTROVERT	17
11	ISOLATION	19
12	CHILDCARE	20
13	MISS HOOD	21
14	APPETITE	23
15	INHERITANCE	25
16	QUESTIONNAIRE	27
17	SOUNDINGS	29
18	ORCHESTRATION	31
19	REALISATION	32
20	EIRWEN	33
21	WELCOME FELT	35
22	IMAGE	38
23	MEMORIES	40
24	COURTESY CODE	42
25	AMBIVALENCE	44
26	UNHEEDING	45
27	DISORDER	47
28	PARASITE	48
29	COCONUT MOMENTS	50

30	FIREPLACE	52
31	BEAUTY	54
32	MORTALITY	55
33	REFLECTION	56
34	PLAYING THE GAME	58
35	BESTRIDERS	60
36	HEIRLOOM	62
37	PINNACLE	64
38	DUE PROCESS	67
39	APHRODITE	69
40	WILD FLOWERS	70
41	NOMENCLATURE	72
42	DECEPTION	74
43	HERMAPHRODITES	76
44	PERSONAL BEST	78
45	ANGEL	79
46	SUN DISCIPLES	80
47	LEA BAILEY	82
48	SCULPTURE TRAILS	84
49	BEAUTIFUL GAME	87
50	INTELLIGENCE	91
51	CARTOGRAPHY	94
52	SHIP OF STATE	95
53	CENOTAPH	97
54	PROPOSAL	98
55	PROPHECY	100
56	ADJACENT SEAT	102
57	CLAPPING	104
58	TACTILE	106
59	DEEP SLEEP	108
60	CASTING VOTE	110

61	OPTING OUT	112
62	DEAD RECKONING	114
63	ELBOW LANE	116
64	WHO'S WHO	118
65	INEVITABILITY	120
66	TONGUE	122
67	THIS LANGUAGE	124
68	COFFEE SHOP	126
69	AM and PM	128
70	HUMAN RESOURCES	130
71	WEDLOCK	131
72	PREROGATIVE	132
73	PRINCE PHILIP'S FUNERAL	134
74	LAUGHTER	135
75	CAMERA	136
76	HOLDING HANDS	138
77	COVID CHRISTMAS 2020	140
78	EU TRADE TALKS 2020	142
79	PASS IT ON	144
80	EURO '2020'	146
81	SCHADENFREUDE	148
82	STEREOTYPES	150
83	BEST FRIEND	152
84	LEADING MAN	154
85	FAVOURITISM	156
86	LITTER	158
87	POMPEY	160
88	THOROUGHBRED	162
89	STREETWISE	164
90	CUSTOMER	166
91	SUSCEPTIBILITY	169

92	ECKS	171
93	GULLWAY BAY	174
94	HELPER	176
95	KNEE-TAKING	177
96	CHILD'S EYES	179
97	ONE TO TEN	180
98	'ISMS'	182
99	TOKYO OLYMPICS	184
100	HONOURS	187
101	NEIGHBOURS	189
102	SOUND EFFECTS	192
103	PROPRIETY	194
104	STANDING STONES	196
105	HISTORY LESSON	198
106	DEVELOPMENT	200
107	DELIVERANCE	204
108	CONUNDRUM	205
109	RESTLESS APPARITION	207
110	SWEET REAPER	209
111	BURIAL	210

Foreword

With the exception of two or three, which were conceived several years earlier, these reflections date from 2019 to 2021.

I had written 'Anthem for England' in 2016 – not to replace the UK anthem – but to give English teams their own anthem to sing at international matches, to counter those of Ireland, Scotland and Wales. However, it is at least as much by music as by words that an anthem rallies a nation, and I could find no one to compose rousing music.

It seems a paradox, but it could be said that when you leave school your education begins. Trite, perhaps, but life is an ongoing kind of education for which, we hope, your schooling has thoroughly prepared you. Who am I to advise you? A valid question: My education has been very patchy, better than many I dare say, but worse than most.

Each of our lives is a kind of personal Odyssey of the mind, and this book is a sifting of my experience as a lifelong introvert. Opinions are worthy of their name; certainties rather less so. We the inhibited, the tongue-tied, are pleased to turn to written words, to join the general discourse, indulge in candid exposure without, I hope, slipping too deeply into self-pity, putting forward our thoughts and opinions like this as Deputies, in lieu of personality.

APPEAL

As my first line, this will have to serve:
The line I had intended, deserted me,
And often, the most eloquent lines
Are the missing ones, promising,
But keeping out of sight,
Sentiments embryonic,
Seldom being brought to term,
However much intended.

Elusive lines must serve some purpose
In remaining so; more, one would hope,
Than sheer cussedness. It could be
They are benign, and kindly of spirit;
A little playful and teasing, maybe.
Well, I don't mind teasing,
Up to a point, but you can take it too far.

A writer might be searching for lines
So charged with insight, and substance—
Lines which generations to come
Will study and memorise—
The quoting of which will
Sustain and fortify through difficult years.
So it's not a teasing matter, really;
I take a rather dim view
Of this aloofness, playing hard to get;
It rather defeats the purpose
Of interesting Literature.

I suppose all I can do is
To appeal to their better nature—
Lending themselves to searchers such as I,
Never to be shy of striking
Sparks of inspiration from us—
Felicitous phrases, resounding tones of
Voice, searching with us in our quest—
In the patient hope of which,
As my last for now, this will have to serve.

SUBJECTIVITY

How we embellish them,
All our words and phrases,
When we utter and hold forth with them:
How we embellish them
With many a gesture, modulate
By tone of voice, expression of face,
Highlighting with our eyes,
With all the heft of heritage,
The dialect, vernacular,
The very rhythms in our speech—
Be they words of tenderness or rage,
My, how we embellish them!

But when we come to write them down,
Print them on some lifeless paper,
Of all embellishments isolated,
Abandoned, utterly shorn—
Felicitous usage, punctuation,
Their only hopes of keeping faith;
Otherwise inanimate, inert,
Remaining filed, shelved or archived,
Silent as notations on the stave,
As though in latent hibernation.

And when it chances, by and by,
That should a reader wander by
To stir those dormant creatures,
How much of what comprised those words,
How much of their intentions,
What chance the writer's very thoughts
Can ever be revived?

The likelihood of kindred thoughts
Is in the minds of kindred sorts—
Those dormant words, limbo frozen
The very words they would have chosen,
Leaving them in little doubt
About that most perceptive writer.

Less inclined to share his views,
Less inclined to follow his thoughts,
Other readers would have chosen
Other words than he had used,
Leaving them in little doubt
About that mediocre writer.

For, shorn of his embellishments,
Now, these words are theirs—
Embellishments are theirs—
And all their personal trappings now
Revitalise his words.

And how we test those stepping-stones
Across from writer to his reader—
Mind to word to page, page to mind—
Is only viewed through hindsight,
All our scholarly debates
About a writer's motivations,
So inescapably subjective,
For in studying works of Literature,
In examining a writer's words and thoughts,
We simply examine ourselves.

CROW

If you have observed, you will know
That every time a carrion crow
'Karks', utters, vocalises,
It really does mean it—
Every gargling syllable of it—
In a whole straining-body blast.
You will have noticed, too,
That his audience, usually
Of one, stays silent;
She has heard it all before,
And it makes no more sense now
Than it has every other time.

It may be, but who knows?
This apparently meaningless karking
Is nothing but the vilest, most
Disgusting language known to crows—
Hardly surprising in a solitary,
Avian scavenger who relishes
Nothing more than picking over
Stinking, putrid carrion.

Or it may be that, for his mate,
Endowed with the same endearing manners,
This torrent of grated noise
Is the most appropriate mating call.

Here, within our own Aviary,
The occasional carrion crow
Is not unknown, strutting noisily
About, with a mouth full of
Foul language, outspokenness
And self-confidence way ahead
Of his talent, or his wisdom:
He makes me so grateful for
Those who speak in gentle tones,
In words of pleasant eloquence
And sincerity, our lyrical people,
Our song thrushes, blackbirds and warblers.

WORC

This is the Author speaking.
I have just received a message
From a most indignant Hen Crow,
Taking exception to something I wrote.
When we of human kind assume
The moral high ground, we never
Know whose toes or claws we tread upon.
I thought I should pass the message
On to you, without comment, translated
From the Corvid, as best I may:

"I've never heard such puffed-up,
Myopic, anthropomorphic Tosh.
Let me take your silly, puerile poem
Point by fatuous point:
When we 'vocalise', as you stuffily
Refer to it, yes, we really do
Mean it, for our calls are pared
Down to sweet facts, bare truths,
From ages past, stripped clean of all
Dissembling and all coarse humanoid
Cursing. How many of you say
What you mean? And what should
It matter to us, that you find
Our voices grating? Our calls make
Perfect sense. How dare you suggest
That, unintelligible to you,
We must be deaf to our own kind?
Our language is way beyond yours;

You lot are too recent, too callow,
Too shallow, ever to understand.
And how dare you refer to your
Noisy, bragging no-hopers
As carrion crows?

"And let me tell you, carrion
Is first-class wholesome food,
Ideal for raising healthy, fledgling crows.
And we do a useful job, too,
Cleaning up the corpses.
You eat mountains of dead meat,
Pigs and cows and poultry, but—
You poor, delicate dears – you
Must have it all cooked! And your
Precious bellies have to have
Specially treated water.
"My dear fellow (the translation's
a bit uncertain there), you can't
Even grow your own fur or feathers—
But you must drape your
Shameful, balding bodies in skins
From countless herds of cattle,
And wool you scrape from flocks of sheep.
You, who depend on the eggs of
Hens, and who make so little of
Your own milk that you rely
Upon herds of dairy cows—

So dependent upon the rest of us
That we are bound to ask,
Just where is your lofty perch
That you look down on 'others'
As 'lessers' or 'lowers'?
Forgive me if my 'tones' are not
Gentle or eloquent enough for you—
Just take off that human blindfold."

NURSERY RHYME

That infant days have served her well,
Is plain for all the world to see,
In the trusting look and the faithful eyes:
She dwells in the land of the truthful word,
Where what's believed is what is heard—
Perhaps a little too naïve,
She's more than likely to believe—
But she must have been a cuddled child.

She dwells in the land of the grown-up child,
Born to pass it down the line,
To be so set and fortified
Against the world's most testing tides,
Remaining firmly at the helm,
Where sorrows threat to overwhelm—
With joy and sadness reconciled,
She must have been a cuddled child.

And so she flowers, with the warmth of friends,
Where a promise made is a promise kept.
She thrives in the land of the helping hand,
As though in a land of sisters and brothers
Where it's less for yourself and more for others—
Much less of takes, much more of gives,
This is the land where the lady lives
Who must have been a cuddled child.

SOU' WESTERLY

Old Sou' Westerly, do as you please;
Do as you've always done before,
These several million years or more.

Familiar, warm Atlantic friend,
Send us your besieging seas;
Drench us, buffet us by all means.
But swell our lakes and green our fields,
Prevailing only to be kind—
A North Atlantic state of mind.

Old Sou' Westerly, do as you please;
Take no notice when we curse:
Easterlies are so much worse.

We recognise you, ancient friend,
Who forged and fed this ancient land:
Old Sou' Westerly's rugged isles—
Temperate, understated isles —
A fitting place, the very place,
To raise and shape a British race.

THE ENGLISH WAY

From Valentine's Day to Easter Eggs,
Country Fairs to Carnival Queens,
Harvest Home to Fireworks Night,
Mistletoe and Christmas Day—
The customary English year
Recites the way we do things here.

Reasons deep in days gone by,
Rituals now, to steer us by—
Whereof tradition never fails;
The breeze to fill the people's sails—
The customary English year
Recites the way we do things here.

Much that we think, we will not say,
Because it's not the English way;
Better be quiet, and persevere;
It's just the way we do things here.
And do not write the month before the day:
Not May the First; the First of May—
It's day, then month, then year;
It's just the way we do things here.

And Honour lies in taking part,
Far more than in the winning:
For the runners-up, the heartiest cheer—
It's just the way we do things here.

Men behave as if they know
It's womenfolk who run the show:
Revealed in Pantomime every year—
Who is the Doddery Dame, but he;
Who the Principal Boy, but she—
It's just the way we do things here.

Male or female, feeble or strong,
Petty, magnanimous, right or wrong—
From Valentine's to Christmas Day,
We do things here the English way.

VOLUNTEERS

Across the shires, in village halls,
Through charities and churches,
Jumble-sales, quizzes and fêtes—
Wherever the country meets or celebrates—
Behind the scenes or manning the stalls,
Stalwart stand the volunteers.

And all we can offer are homespun cheers,
For homespun, they are volunteers.

It is as though, deep down
In the British way of life,
There runs an aquafer of fellow-feeling,
Imbibed through thirsty generations—
Cultivating helpers,
Cultivating helpers.

And all we can offer are homespun cheers,
For homespun, they are volunteers.

Come pestilence or floods,
Come loss or hunger or drought,
Benevolent instincts in our midst
Hardly need be called for—
It'll not be long before someone
You've never spoken to, nor known,
Is at your side, as one of your own.

And all we can offer are homespun cheers,
For homespun, they are volunteers.

There is, for them, no higher reward
Than the satisfaction of being kind:
Full payment in itself, in kind.

They'll be embarrassed enough by homespun cheers,
But you will see them sometimes
Added on to an Honours List,
Rather like an afterthought.
For as it should be, in an Honours List,
The honour bestowed was never sought.

ANTHEM FOR ENGLAND

'Loyal Hearts'

Safe in loyal English hearts,
Freedoms won are here to stay;
Safe in loyal English hands,
Freedoms none shall take away.

Our thanks to Dear Old England,
And the courage of the people,
Cottage and farm and village and town,
For all our freedoms handed down.

Never doubt we shall defend
The English way, and freedom's way:
Ever knowing right from wrong,
The weak protected by the strong,
A trusted word and a helping hand,
England, our ancestral land.

INTROVERT

In the dining-hall one day, silently
Enjoying my meal, while listening, with
Interest, to the banter around the table
I was stopped, by one well-bred fellow
Turning to include me, by inviting
My opinion: All eyes turned and
Looked for my response, which made it
Worse; I could only manage some
Embarrassed mumbling, of not really
Having an opinion, while avoiding eye-contact.

I had an opinion, of course, plenty
Of opinions, but with so little 'presence',
Personality or self-confidence, even then,
In my thirties, to put opinions forth.
It was one of many consequences
Of my being ill-equipped and
Ill-prepared by background—
Never issued, as it were, with
A voice, raised to be subordinate,
Intrinsically passive, to this day.

And to this day, if I have
A choice of where to sit,
In a pub or restaurant,
It will be a corner, or by a wall.

I once heard it said, that since
We have two ears, and only one
Mouth, it behoves us to listen
Twice as much as we speak.
I think it was intended as a
Brake on the garrulous, but
I took some comfort from it.

I was to find that Amateur
Dramatics, and now, writing,
Were natural resorts, and
'Outlets' for the tongue-tied.
And thus it would seem to follow
That I write at least as much
For my own purposes, as for
The interest and considerations
Of any future readers.

ISOLATION

The boy had been adequately clothed, and shod,
And seldom had he lacked for food,
Yet somehow was naked, and starved.

He wore his features as a mask;
A bland, anonymous face,
Drawn over, like some carapace.

When he was missing, he might be found,
Had anybody searched,
In some passageway, spare room, corner,
Wanting to cry, knowing not why:
Sobbing, silently, to himself—
Silently, that no one might hear—
If anyone would be listening.

Where were his mother and father?
Had he no mother nor father?
Why cries he not out loud?

Has no one noticed him?
Let's hope not, in a charitable way—
For who could notice him, and turn away?

If no angel of mercy comes by,
Likely he'll cry for the rest of his days,
Never quite hidden, from public gaze:
An oddity, with very few friends,
Adequately clothed, shod, and fed—
His only use for a begging-bowl,
Some loving sustenance for his soul.

CHILDCARE

It's not always possible, we know,
To be a loving mother to a child,
But where we can, we surely must—
For what can give that child more heart
Than a firm and homely, motherly start?
No higher calling can there be;
Why settle for anything less?

It's not always possible, we know,
But where we can, we surely must—
However high you may aspire,
Nothing, ever, can be higher;
No better contribution to mankind
Than mothering, in this old world—
Why settle for anything less?

This whole wide world is our child
(Who was not to a mother born?):
What can give this world more heart,
Than a firm and homely, motherly start?

And when this whole wide world cries,
We know one sad reason why:
We hear those cries, and we hazard a guess,
That maybe for far too long,
We've been settling for anything less.

MISS HOOD

I first heard the good news
When I was four-and-a-half,
Starting at infants' school:
She stood before us, our Miss Hood,
No more than two-and-twenty then,
Looking back, I'd say.

"Hands together, eyes closed," she said,
For chanting the morning prayer—
She might as well have said
"Minds together, minds closed,
Or you'll never believe what follows"—
Looking back, I'd say.

The son, of a supernatural father,
Is cruelly put to death—
But soon comes back to life,
So that we may live forever,
If we believe in Him.
No doubt, at four or five years old,
Miss Hood believed what she was told,
Looking back, I'd say.

Pages seven and eight, I had to read
When my turn came, in Reading Time:
"GOOOOOD!" blessed she, with her angel smile—
Imprinted then, and evermore, within me,
Forever mine in time of need—
The comfort of our Miss Hood's blessing,
In my memory's eyes and ears.

How such a force for goodness rides
Upon such improbable tides,
May have been beyond Miss Hood,
But it was as if she understood
The value of such tidings,
Looking back, I'd say.

Wherein lay the wonderful news
Promised in those infant days?
Looking back, I'd say those moments of praise,
The fathomless reach of appreciative words
From Miss Hood, and all of her sort,
To every child, ever they taught.

APPETITE

Our father did not dine; he fed:
Hunched over his plate as if to guard it,
Like some raptor at its kill,
That had to be protected—
So urgent was our father's need;
Our father did not dine; he fed.

Before the scraps were taken away,
He'd be relishing his duff—
Main courses never quite enough;
You never know when the next will be—
So urgent was our father's need
Not so much to dine, as feed.

Little, back then, did we understand
What by and by was plain to see:
Our father did not feed alone—
Other feeders being fed:
Wherever lurked or roosted they,
Certain memories found no rest;
Some old perturbances of mind
Raised hungers of a different kind—

As we would only comprehend,
Well after we had flown his nest.

And now we too, tried, found wanting,
With nameless troubles on our minds:
Feeding with our thoughts elsewhere,
Reaching for an extra helping,
Feeling, as our father must have felt,
The eyes of watching children,
The eyes of children watching,
Little understanding, yet noticing.

INHERITANCE

My mother-to-be was illegitimate;
Unsanctioned, misbegotten, you see;
Though 'Every beast of the earth'
'And every fowl of the air', and
'Every thing that creepeth upon the earth'
And everything that God had made
Was very good, legitimate, it would seem,
My mother-to-be was illegitimate;
Unsanctioned, misbegotten:
Sent to a foster-home, fatherless and motherless—
Learned to be grateful and disciplined—
Perfunctorily schooled, taught her duties;
Fitted for employment in domestic service.

She married a soldier, in due course,
And I am legitimate, you see,
Though my mother-to-be
Had no particular need of me:
Dutifully, she brought us up,
With no more affection than she had ever known.

Dutifully, on meagre allowance,
She fed and clothed us, told us
To be good, gave us medicines,
Hid sixpences in each
Of our Christmas puddings,
And shielded us from father—
But affection, warmth and joy
Bare duty never can dispense.

No one ever knew my mother,
A living, breathing instrument—
A means of having things done properly:
Closeness she could never bear —
"Go on, y'dopey Daniel", her scullery echo
To "Run along now, there's a dear".

We ran along, as early as we could,
Square pegs all, failed marriages all,
Sentenced to Life, of inward strife:
I pass it on, for what it's worth—
Legacy of lovelessness
Upon some misbegotten birth.

QUESTIONNAIRE

Life did seem simpler in those days,
So neatly defined were we,
Filling in Forms and Questionnaires.

I had to have a sex, one or the other—
Put 'M' or 'F', or cross out the wrong one.

They asked me for my Date of Birth
And then, just to be sure,
They asked what age I was.

I had to have a Next of Kin, it said:
That was always your Dad,
Or your Mum if your Dad was dead.

I had to have a Religion.
'You're Church of England',
Said my Mum, 'Just put C of E';
I didn't know I had a Religion
Until my mother told me.
Back then, everyone had Christian Names;
Now it's First Names, so not to offend.

And, as a useful citizen in the making,
I had to have Hobbies—
Always, there was a space for Hobbies:
Say stamp-collecting, meccano, bird-watching,
Balsa-wood modelling, scouting – as many
As I could answer questions on, at Interview.

I had to have appropriate Sports—
Football, rugby, cricket expected for boys—
Hockey, netball, tennis more seemly for girls.

I had to have Ambitions—
What I wanted to be, when I grew up,
And what the reasons were
In case they asked me, at Interview.
I was a male, Christian, scouting footballer, who
Wanted to join the Navy.

Forms had to be verified, or countersigned
By some pillar of society—
A Minister of Religion, a Doctor or MP,
Even though he scarcely knew me,
Or had never heard of me.

When I left home, Mum said, 'Be Good';
Dad said, 'Keep your mouth shut and
Do as you're told'.

SOUNDINGS

One wonders at our stillness here,
That we can be so moved to tears—
Involuntary, released on our behalf,
Revealed, in spite of ourselves.
As far apart as joy and sadness,
Yet kindred are their tears,
Embarrassing, betraying us;
Distillation, it would seem,
Of essence we would rather hide,
Something tender, touched inside.

From just what finer filaments
Are we so strung that we must hide—
Some shame of baser instincts?
Denial of a heritage?
All our learned lexicons,
Our best poetic turns of phrase,
Will splash along our shores —
But take soundings of our stillness
Anywhere near our ocean floor,
What else be music made for?

Not so much hid, perhaps, as unheard,
And how necessary to be heard,
That so precisely would we craft
And fashion ourselves biddable puppets,
Of rhythm, of brass, and woodwinds,
And marionettes of strings,
Whereto, with endless practice and persuasion,
Plead ourselves, confess ourselves,
Stir the stillness, in spite of ourselves,
Work such alchemy at our ears,
Raise to the surface a truth, in tears.

ORCHESTRATION

Oh, Euterpe! Muse of Dionysian music,
Patroness of joy and pleasure—
As one of your Devotees, I plead
A new consideration:
Having to navigate stormy seas,
I must have been easier to please,
Finding an anchorage more to my needs
Than to my temperament—
Echoing with such tocsin chimes
From your loud and clamorous parts,
Cymbals, Timpani and Brasses.

Forgive me, Patroness, if now I call—
Now that the seas are calmer,
Now that the harbour lies in sight—
A loving call, to woodwinds now, and strings,
A lady of lyrical sensibilities—
More thoughtful music in her soul,
Softer to my nerves and senses,
Full of loving, tender feelings—
Rendered best in woodwinds, and in strings.

REALISATION

Our tenderest feelings are apt themselves to hide away,
As if to avoid the searching light of day,
And being truths essential, from our deepest well,
Where be any means, these truths to tell?
Beyond the scope, it seems, of all nine Muses,
What chance a mortal, whatever words he chooses?
For while feelings cannot help arising,
Words be merely artefacts, deputising—
Invented as our servants, handmaids at our call—
What chance they, to tell such truths at all?
Weave them how he may, to flush his feelings out of cover,
Yet may they fall short, in the senses of his lover.

One wonders if at all, or perhaps how best,
Tender feelings can be rendered manifest:
And so I put words forth, as best I may,
That what I feel might see the light of day,
And blinking in this unaccustomed light,
Be welcomed, known, acknowledged, in your sight—
That as my love is recognised, and known,
You see a true and clear reflection of your own.

EIRWEN

To say that she is always on my mind,
Would be absurd, as if nothing else
Had been on my mind through all
The intervening years. But her very
Name itself, 'Eirwen', especially heard
In her own Welsh lilt, is ever present
Within me, and has echoed throughout
My life— just such a memory, I would guess,
Residing in the minds of so many men.
For she it was, who first kindled,
At my adolescence, that which
Was impatient for the kindling.
That weather-worn and elusive word
'Love' would not do, though I'm sure,
At the earliest, tenderest of touches
In those days, I felt it so.

Notwithstanding the very different
Paths we took, on leaving school,
Her imprint was within me.
It seems that we encountered
Comparable fortunes, and misfortunes,
And when our paths did cross again,
In later middle age, it was
Entirely by chance, yet how tempting
To fancy some guiding principle—
For her imprint was within me.

But if intimations such as these
Are flights for poetry,
Life is roughed out in prose.
Few are those Prospects that
Retrospect will never bring to heel:
One of life's paradoxes, maybe—
Somehow sad that we never wed;
Just as well that we never did,
Though indelible, her imprint within me.

In our old age now, exchanging
Christmas cards feels entirely apt—
Signed off with two or three
Festive X's, representing kisses—
What-might-have-been, wistful kisses,
For the girl I lost across the years,
Young Eirwen, my old Welsh friend.

WELCOME FELT

For all the vagaries of chance and choice
That led to my arrival here,
To this, my penultimate resting-place,
Along Lea Bailey's watery end,
I am sincerely thankful.

First and foremost, it is the people:
I have yet to meet an unpleasant person
In this whole neighbourhood
Where Herefordshire touches Gloucestershire—
Neighbours all, by name and nature,
Living proof of local history,
For such hospitable people
Can only be descendants
Of such a robust ancestry,
In many generations gone by,
Who took hardship in their stride,
Learned to work for the common good,
Shook you by the hand, looked you in the eye
And asked, "How bist, old Butt?"

I was surrounded, from the outset,
By a charm of Words — Pudding Hill,
Flaxley, Plump Hill, Knights Hill,
Puddlebrook, May Hill, Wigpool,
East Dean, Mitcheldean, Dean Common Farm—
And what am I to make of Dancing Green?

I will not hear of historical truths;
Tedious facts impertinent, out of order:
It must have been, surely still, it is
An enchanted space, where human spirits
Quite unseen, tryst and dance with fairy lovers,
Making wishes, stealing kisses
On magical summer evenings.

Perhaps I should have said 'Names', not 'Words',
For our ancestors, mostly, could neither
Read nor write, yet with their footprints,
Their fingerprints, their imaginations,
They have signed themselves upon the land.
We know that their lives were lives of toil—
Forestry, quarrying, mining for iron ore,
Mining for coal, farming, cloth-making,
Leather-working, charcoal-burning, blacksmithery—
And the bearing, oh, the birthing of their babies,
Against appalling odds of infant mortality.

They seemed to make the most of things,
With celebrations, fairs and carnivals,
All in the bosom of the Christian Church,
Offering inspiration, comfort, purpose and Hope—
Hope! Who has not walked hand-in-hand
With Hope? We have Longhope here,
With a church of Norman beginnings,
We have Flaxley where, in the 12th century,
Stood a Cistercian monastery,
We've the 14th century St Michael's church,
Which gave its name to Mitcheldean;

St Michael's too, in Hope Mansell,
With traces from the 12th century,
And whose 'Hope' is noted
In the Domesday Book.
Traces of Christianity, from medieval,
Norman, even Saxon times.
And since the Reformation,
Anglican, Baptist, Methodist worshippers
As well, knit our parishes together.

Wherever they find their inspiration,
It is all the local people, and their
Practical common sense, gleaned
Not so much from books as from
The lives of those around them;
It is their kindness, natural intuition,
Their sense of what is right,
Investing in their children all the
Loving guidance, best advice;
It is all the local people, their welcome,
And their proud inheritance,
That I am so grateful for:
If any were to ask how I bist, I'd say
"Proper lucky now, thanks old Butt".

IMAGE

Since there is no one to tell our tale,
But we ourselves, it may be flawed,
And should be questioned—
But whom are we to ask?

Primates, we call ourselves—
Of all the mammals, all the vertebrates,
Primates, along with monkeys and the apes—
Hence Hominidae, our human family,
And now Homo, sole survivor—
Species 'sapiens', we shamelessly claim,
Embodying a kind of truth,
Though Homo 'narcissusens'
Might have been more truthful still,
Whereof our dawning thoughts were spawned,
Whereof a nakedness was born.

Nor fleece, nor hide, nor pelt—
But skin, vulnerable, naked skin,
For even on the hottest days,
With all our brazen skin displays,
Clothing covers just how far
Detached from natural, sleek, alert we are—

But when we are unclothed, exposed,
On whom can civilised man depend,
To whom for naked truth appeal
But Mirror, candid confidante and friend?
I doubt we could live in a Mirrorless world:
Throughout our lives she watches us
In that silent and impartial way,
Allowing us to see ourselves,
But left for right and right for left—

Never, never a day goes by
Without we and Mirror, eye to eye;
Sixty thousand consultations
In a lifetime, that would make,
Be it only twice a day.
And Mirror– we just know her—
More than sees; she positively stares:
It is one thing to be naked,
Another to be aware of it,
Exposed at mind as well as skin,
Not only to people's eyes,
But to their thoughts as well.
Mirror has those watching thoughts,
As well as staring eyes,
Knowing more than we would wish,
As if she could very well be
Telling our tale, more truthfully than we.

MEMORIES

What wouldn't I give, to be able to choose
Which memories keep, and which to lose—
Involuntary as they are, partaking of us,
Intruding uninvited in our thoughts—
And in my particular, introspective case,
However much I've obliged, or enhanced;
Whatever benefits bestowed, kindness shown,
Conscience will not set me free
From memories embarrassing,
Outweighing those which comfort me.

I wish there were more things
About myself that pleased me—
I failed too many tests:
Slow-wittedness, incompetence,
Memories may forgive,
But foolish acts and comments,
Falling short of tact or taste,
Will never let the conscience rest.
May they not persist in others' minds,
As persist in mine, undiminished over time.

Acts and comments foolish—
Tactless, tasteless, yes, of course.
Yet never malicious, I dearly hope;
Thoughtless, never heartless,
I can't be sure, but dearly wish
I'd find some means, within my mind,
Of sifting out good memories,
And leaving other ones behind:
Full King's Ransom would I pay,
To flush those memories away.

COURTESY CODE

Driving on the open road,
On business or on pleasures,
On carriageways or country lanes;
Rather like a vital stream,
We keep the country ticking over,
Flowing through the country's veins.
And further to the Highway Code,
We keep it well the only way:
The unofficial courtesy code;
The Fellowship of the Road.

It calls for understanding,
Out on the open road;
Making do with silent signs
Behind the windscreen, at the wheel:
That instinctive smile, that wave,
That lifted-fingers "thankyou" at the wheel—
Courtesies all as pleasing
To give as to receive—
The unofficial courtesy code;
The Fellowship of the Road.

Anonymous as these gestures are—
For we seldom see the face—
They are valued that much more
For what they signify:
Fellowship in the public space.
Passing by, untouching,
They touch us none the less,
And we're all the better for it:
The unofficial courtesy code;
The Fellowship of the Road.

AMBIVALENCE

Without the instinct to preserve itself,
There is no life; our nature
Is to be self-serving; that's all
There is, inherent, at our core.

And yet, in our common discourse,
While some insist 'Look after Number One',
Selfishness is widely disapproved,
In favour of charity and kindness;
At odds with ourselves, it seems—
Domesticated man, in spite of himself.
Benevolence and Avarice; I wonder
Which better fits us for the world.

And what a moralising journey made,
From early days, when 'snitching'
Was unforgiveable, and breaking Rules
A badge of merit; who wants
To be known as 'Goody Two-Shoes'?

Maturing to know better, but some
Can be too saintly for public ease,
While too many others take the criminal line,
Where 'snitching' toughens to 'grassing-up'.

Somehow, tacitly, we settle for a norm,
A least uncomfortable contradiction—
Venality or Saintliness, I wonder
Which better fits us for the world.

UNHEEDING

We cannot say we were not forewarned,
But Cassandra-like, our prophet was ignored;
Our elected leaders would not listen
To such irrational fears.

Some Form it was, I had to complete,
Some Form, oh, thirty-odd years ago,
Required to know my 'ethnicity'—
Whereof was my native place,
Where located in the human race.
The nearest thing was 'white/Caucasian'.
I had to look it up: The Caucasus—
Mountainous patchwork of peoples,
Between the Black and Caspian seas;
It seems I'm inseparable from these.

Actually, I am not from there—
I'm thoroughly English, and British,
But 'Caucasian' is a badge I have to wear.
I feel no more Caucasian than Asian,
And charming though Caucasians may well be,
The Caucasus is not quite me.

It was as if, with fifty-year-long yawns,
Governments rubbed their misty eyes,
Awakening with some fake surprise
To a land of new ethnicities,
Saw a land not so much cohering—

Just as Cassandra had forewarned—
But separating out, race by race,
Culture by culture jostling,
About as mixable as oil and water—
And thought it might be worthwhile
To start enumerating, monitoring,
Seeming to think these numbers matter.

Oh, but they matter so pressingly now:
Prophetic warnings all unheeded,
Governments have given us, the voters,
No voice, no choice but accept
This intractable mess
We never wanted, never asked for, nor needed.

DISORDER

The toilet-roll has room to slide
Each way a little along its holder.
If, on a visit, finding it at one end,
You instinctively nudge it central,
I extend to you my sympathy,
As a blighted comrade-in-thrall.

"How neat and tidy you keep it all",
A visitor will say,
As though to pay a compliment—
All things in their allotted place,
Items level and symmetrical,
Parallel or in line—
No need for me to say "Excuse the mess".
Not virtue this, they've come upon,
But life constrained and circumscribed;
Not virtue this, but helplessness,
Possessed by some fastidious demon:

If our pictures must be horizontal,
Our books parade in rank and file
Ready for inspection;
If restlessly our mind rehearses
The freeing of a curtain,
The straightening of a cushion
Until we 'ups and does it',
It is not compliments we need,
But gentle, soothing therapy.

PARASITE

This instinctual beast to which we cling—
Unself-conscious, unaware,
With no capacity to think,
Seems to know a thing or two—
Simply munches what tastes good,
Slaking deep of what refreshes,
Knows which way are food and drink.

This instinctual beast to which we cling,
Scratches itself when it itches,
Only fights a winnable fight,
Licking clean its cuts and scrapes;
Bellows and howls to vent its feelings,
Relieves itself right here and now,
Sleeps when it's tired and safe.

This instinctual beast to which we cling,
Has no concept of tomorrow,
Yet seems to know a thing or two:
At restless seasons of the year,
From odd posturings, displays,
Scentings and presentings
Compulsive couplings will ensue—
Without a thought or state of mind,
Routinely replicates its kind.

This instinctual beast to which we cling,
Would do just fine without us:
What beast ever needed thoughts?
Or politics? Or plans?
For all the good we do,
We might as well play games,
Paint pictures, sing songs and dance;
And I guess we could do worse
Than writing sundry lines of verse.

COCONUT MOMENTS

Loitering, at the Lea Village Summer Fete,
I found myself manning the coconut stall,
Handing out the rings, taking the cash,
While my friend was taking a comfort break—
When along came a fellow, with his son,
"Three rings for the lad, please," said he:
The boy's third ring found its target,
But clung, like a chinstrap,
Across the face of the prize.
"Oh bad luck," said his Dad, "It's got
To go all the way down to the ground"—
While I stood dumbly, unsure of the rules,
Off he went, with the crestfallen boy,
Leaving me privately dying of shame.

Loitering, at the Lane End Church Fete,
Having a go at this stall and that,
Entering into the spirit of things,
I watched a young girl at the coconut stall—
Missing, with all three of her rings:
 When my turn came, to my surprise,
I wandered away with a coconut prize.
And after a while, whom should I see,
But that young girl who missed with all three.
"Would you like a coconut?" said I;
Alarmed, she uttered no reply
But flustered, and flushing up red,
Recoiled from me, and fled.

I was a strange man offering gift to a child:
How well was she advised, to turn and flee,
Yet how sad to have to tell a child
That kindness offered, may not kindness be.

I wish I could find that boy,
To present him with his prize,
And to his Dad, belatedly apologise.
And congratulate that girl's Mum and Dad,
For arming her with such caution,
Though such caution be so sad.
For myself, I'd wish the personality
To cope and act spontaneously,
To sense the best, and make it so,
In moments such as these—
As not to loiter in the minds
Of that young boy, that young girl,
And, of course, in mine.

FIREPLACE

Sitting before an open fire
Is sitting in a kind of trance:
Nothing mesmerises minds,
Or quite beguiles the idle gaze,
As surrendering one's mind
To the spell of an open fire.

'We meet again', it seems to thrum,
In strange, familiar tune,
Less to the ears than to the soul;
'We meet again', it seems to whisper,
Hissing, flickering tongues—
Primitive patois, intuitively felt—
Ingested through our trusting pores.
Oddly charmed, we watch it kindle,
Eagerly grow, taking hold,
Spreading, heating, gaining
All it may, and then to
Dwindle, fade, and end,
Depleted, still, and cold.

For, met before, of course we have,
Since first we learned to conjure flames—
And how to douse them out—
To huddle together for their heat,
To warm our feet, scorch our meat.
We learned it as a friend,
But fickle friend, as soon as welcomes,
Warns us off; not too close;
Keep respectful distance—
And what kind of friend
Comforts only as we feed it?
What kind of friend
Has no purpose but its own?

Wary then, and deliver us then
From mesmerising spells like those:
A meeting, not surrendering, of minds;
A kindling, but of mutual friends—
And ever let those friendships burn
Which ask for nothing in return.

BEAUTY

Beauty, in our human race, stands quite alone;
Intrinsic so, it's quite itself,
'Beauty' cannot be applied:
There is no such thing as a beautiful face
Without a beautiful mind inside,
Without a gracious spirit inside.

Notwithstanding your classical features,
Cheek bones, noble brows and jawline,
Eyes and mouth in true proportion—
Your face will be a vacant place;
Sterile, each attempted smile,
Without a gracious spirit inside.

Your nose can never be too long,
Never too close together your eyes,
Nor too far one way, your mouth,
That beauty cannot animate,
And through your features radiate
A generous, gracious spirit inside.

No more can beauty be contrived
Than laughter can be fabricated;
Cosmetics can be kind,
But hardly help to beautify the mind.
Beauty is not self-conscious, knows no art:
Needing no quotation marks,
Authentic and spontaneous,
Let's say beauty rises in the heart.

MORTALITY

If you were the Immortal God of all,
Originator, benevolent Creator of all,
Inclined to make images, and likenesses
Of your immortal, benevolent self,
Why on Earth, at their very birth,
Would you guarantee their death?

That the omnipotent Deity would create
A person who must eat, to stay alive,
And so for want of food must starve to death—
A person who must breathe clean air,
And for want of such, must suffocate,
Would seem so very odd.

And what divinely-created Being
Should ever need to sleep?
Or replicate its kind the way we do,
Much the same as all God's creatures do?
Perhaps created so not to feel
Out of place in a merely mortal world?

If you were the Immortal God of all,
Why not make us all saints, instead of sinners?
Leave the subordinate creatures down here,
And in your benevolence keep us likenesses
And images up there with you in Heaven,
Guaranteeing saintly everlasting lives,
Instead of all this Earthbound Travail,
And all these Trials that we may fail?

REFLECTION

Pillage our planet how we may,
Bulldoze habitats how we may,
On any but ourselves laying blame—
For are we not divinely authorised,
Over fish and fowl, every living thing,
To have dominion?
I doubt Genesis, these days, is widely read,
But it seems, from old susceptible days,
Inherit we a state of mind
Unto ourselves gropingly blind.

Ours a kind of saintly entitlement
Bequeathed upon ourselves:
How many hideous torturings, murderings,
Do we hear condemned as "inhuman",
When, beyond the scope of any other kind,
Exclusively, disgracefully, unmistakeably
Human, is what they are?
Embarrassing ironies abound—
For custodians of all that's right and kind,
Unto ourselves gropingly blind.

Well may we polish our looking-glass,
For a better look at ourselves,
And well may we call for volunteers:
Where ours is the suffering, and
A vaccine needs proving; where better,
More fitting, than upon ourselves?
For the agonies of rats or monkeys
Are no less for being out of sight,
Their convulsions, however muffled,
Ever ringing in our ears.

Well may we polish this looking-glass,
That the more we look the more we see,
And recognise,
The way we are through Nature's eyes,
And to our many human virtues
Let responsibility, humility, be added.

PLAYING THE GAME

Having understood the Rules,
We might wonder why they're there,
Expressing, as they do, merely what is fair.
To be the best that we can be,
We best personify those Rules—
With conscience as our Referee;
What more uplifting for the world to see?
What use an extra Referee?

Having understood the Rules,
This Arbiter inside us all
Should never let our standards fall:
Games and sports seem sent to prove us,
Try us in a public court—
Not quite a capital offence,
But not far short,
To have contempt for Rules, in sport.

Having understood the Rules,
You can be so good at sport—
But never, never, the best,
If you should fail the conscience test.
Sport, to be worthy of its name,
Is more than playing your opponent—
Much more, it's playing the game,
With conscience as your Referee.

Having understood the Rules,
Play for your School, your Club, your County,
When you're sent to represent
Their values, pride and aspirations:
Playing fair, you play for your people—
Win or lose, with a smile on your face—
The very proving of a nation,
And a beacon for the human race.

BESTRIDERS

So common it is, we've long lost sight of it,
Unnoticed because so familiar to see—
To see a person sitting astride a horse,
In complete control of the horse,
Partaking, as it were, of the magnificence,
Of the dignity, poise and strength of the horse:
The horse may not wish to move, nor stop, nor turn;
To trot, to canter, still less to jump,
And yet it does as it is told—
Equus Caballus by Homo Sapiens controlled.

If there is a Forgiver,
May we be forgiven,
For we seem to see nothing to forgive.

Way up here, from our peak and summit,
We cast around, and find no equals—
Nothing around to trouble us much,
To protest, as we validate,
Verify and approve ourselves—
And even consciences do shrink
From promptings inconvenient,
And promptings impertinent—
For anything which magnifies us
Must be honourable, and right.

If there is a Forgiver,
May we be forgiven,
For we seem to see nothing to forgive.

Even those who worship higher spirits
Will capture and corral wild horses,
And feel entitled so to do,
Patiently, methodically, 'break' them,
Castrating them where necessary—
Break their free, wild spirits, breeding out
All independence, and mistrust of us
Until they submit, subordinated—
And suffer our crowning insult
Of sitting proudly astride their backs.

If there is a Forgiver,
May we be forgiven,
For we seem to see nothing to forgive.

"What can be amiss, if the horses love it so?"
Perceptible in this, a faint residual glow
In one of the darkest of our darkling parts,
A rationalising glimmer of conscience,
A long-extinguished light:
"It's nothing new, for heaven's sake—
We've been together, horse and man,
Ages longer than we know:
Were we not for one another made,
Man for horse and horse for man?"

May we be forgiven,
For even now we see nothing to forgive.
It's for sitting, unblushing, on their backs,
That I blush for us all.

HEIRLOOM

Sage Old Spinster, please,
Just what is this thread you spin,
That I must weave upon my loom?

Oh, odds and ends of Space and Time,
Sundry shades of Dark and Light,
Fundamental fibres, elemental strands
Of particles, potential forces,
Left from some primordial age—
Way preceding thought, imagination, word;
Of context or purpose quite unborn—
Materials raw and ready found,
Wherewith the Universe is bound,
I gather to my spinning-wheel.

As I must spin what can be spun,
So must you weave what can be woven.

Sage Old Spinster, please,
Just what is this yarn you tell,
That I must weave upon my loom?

Nay, Madam Weaver, mine is no telling,
Mine no Tale; Spinsters merely spin:
Yours is the yarn, yours the story;
Weave it, embellish it how you will;
Dye it in your earthly hues;
Design, endow it how you choose.
Add whatever value comes your way,
Imprint your fancies and your needs:
Trace your pedigree from on high,
And magnify your kind thereby.

As I must spin what can be spun,
So must you weave what can be woven.

PINNACLE

It is in a language as old as the hills,
That mountain ranges express themselves,
A language not exactly heard
But rather understood, inferred—
All-considered, forbearing and grand,
Enriched with age and wisdom.

Time was, when the local news and views
Around the crags, the valleys and the combes,
Would be exchanged, inferred,
All day through, well into the night—
But now, the daily discourse is suppressed,
By a not entirely welcome guest.

These days, only when the light begins to fade,
And the last of the mountaineers has left—
Tourist, sightseer, hiker, climber, has left—
Can the highs and lows and ridges of the range
Express their wonder, and growing concern for
The travails of the topmost of their peaks.

Most of the hills, of course, have felt
The tread of human feet, but none
More susceptibly, in every mountain range,
Than the slopes of its highest peaks:
Silently, overnight, they attend as she
Recounts the sufferings of her days.

Year by year, the pattern is the same,
But slowly, things are getting worse:
Peaceful the winters, compensating for the cold,
But when the warmth returns, about
The time the raptors and the hares
Are replenishing, and days are growing longer,
So return, as you know, the climbers,
Sometimes around your lesser heights—
But predominantly, by far, something
Draws them to the tallest, proudest peaks,
Needing to reach our very tops—
Not just highest mountain, atop the highest peak.
'Conquering' us, they like to call it,
Invariably choosing the easiest route.
Which after the summer months, seems
To bear the stamp of every climber's boot.

Oblivious to the scars they leave
All up our ancient mountain faces—
And scars not all they leave – litter too,
Imperishable cartons, a bottle here, there a can,
Nor seem they unaware of their fixation,
And the consequences of it all—
Today, they were actually forming queues,
As if their consciences made them pause,
But not much more than pause.

And so, my dear and ancient friends,
It seems that mankind's curious thirst
For 'conquering' our tallest peaks
Is never to be slaked. How, at least,
Are we to understand it?

Deeply silent, deserted by their language
Quite as ancient as their hills,
All the mountain ranges, in all
Their age and wisdom, were dumbfounded,
Human frailty, never to be understood,
Simply wondered at, inferred.

DUE PROCESS

There comes a time in every child's life,
When the beautiful truth has dawned—
Fairly early in the morning,
Even as they're comprehending
Differences, girls from boys—
Out of the fog of fanciful tales,
Out of the thicket of rumours,
Simple, beautiful truth shines though:
Unlike poor little 'Topsy',
Who imagined she simply 'growed',
And 'nobody never made me',
Babies arise from a process of mating.

Then, sure as day must follow night,
And babies, consequent to mating,
There comes that time in every child's life,
That Realisation, that Shock,
That challenge to credulity—
When they ponder their Mother and Father.

It is scarcely to be imagined—
He and she, behave in such a way?
Utterly unlikely; some mistake, must be;
Just look at them; hardly know each other;
Mum does Mum things; Dad, Dad things:
Suppose they must have done.   Jesus.

It's only when the years have done to you,
Roughly what they did to them,
Finding yourself blossomed and ripened
By stages beyond your control,
That you adopt your personal voice, but fall
To that old fundamental call,
And tread that parental pathway—
By choice, of course, if quite involuntary—
Embraced by the beautiful truth of it,
Reflecting, by and by, what will be will be,
Probably with some inkling,
Of what the young children are thinking.

APHRODITE

She reigns, our queenly Aphrodite;
Imagined so, but yet Almighty,
She reigns in our imagined skies,
Wherefrom our love she dignifies.

And so are nature's ways refined,
For we are but the earthly kind.

At her feet it seems we kneel,
Telling lovers how we feel,
All our earthly loves confessing,
With Aphrodite's gentle blessing.

And so are nature's ways refined,
For we are but the earthly kind.

For granting us this heavenly favour,
It would seem just right and fair—
Be Aphrodite so inclined—
That heavenly ways might be refined,
And she could gently sip and savour
Pleasures of the earthly kind.

WILD FLOWERS

Who shall we think we are?
Before we people happened along,
The wild flowers of the world,
Having no need for names,
Had no names;
And having no need for beauty,
Had no beauty—
Each one perfect for its purpose,
No more than its necessary self.

Who shall we think we are?
We granted them Latin and colloquial names,
Dubbing these beautiful; those not so much,
Valuing, delighting in some,
But in others not so much—
Lords and Ladies of the Earth,
Appointed arbiters of worth,
Though each is perfect for its purpose,
No more than its necessary self.

Who shall we think we are
If we so elevate ourselves?
Is not beauty a spurious, human thing,
A temptress and a vanity—
Loyal accomplice of humanity?
And wherein lies the worth
Of our commitment to this Earth,
To be perfect for our purpose,
No more than our necessary selves?

No need to wonder who we are,
If we show forth our necessary selves
For the flowering of mankind—
Not the beauties nor the names
But the attributes themselves,
For which there is such growing need—
Gracious manners, sincerity, and being kind,
As perfect for our purpose
As any cowslip, wood anemone, or garden weed.

NOMENCLATURE

As always, exceptions are to be found,
But how female are the wild flowers!
How aptly, pleasingly female!
Excepting Basil, Ragged Robin
And of course, Herb Robert—
Behold Ladies' Fingers, Lady's Bedstraw,
Lady's Mantle, Lady's Smock—
Flowers and ladies, each of each partake.

Delightful names, evocative names,
Candidly colourful, offering names,
As Violet, Coral and Rose;
Modest and alluring names,
Angelica, Cicely, Myrtle;
Openly flowering, functional names,
Primrose, Lily and Daisy.

So would it not make perfect sense,
To name us conscientious gents,
Who aptly serve as moths and bees,
According to what we have to do,
Alighting to sip and to savour,
Perchance to pollinate, too?

So name our sons Looper or Tussock,
Gipsy, Bumble or Hawk,
Carpenter, Tiger or Heath,
Carder, Mason or Oak—
Entomology, Botany, hand-in-hand,
By providence of spring,
And a million springs foregone,
Brought together in word and deed,
To propagate better our seed.

DECEPTION

Emancipated ladies, please,
Now that you have spread your wings,
May we enter a belated plea:
Forgive us please, and understand
How very much were we deceived.
It came from our fathers, and from theirs,
And theirs, away back then,
When nothing seemed worse than a crowing hen.

You were the gentler, caring ones—
'Sugar and spice and all things nice';
Princesses in the Fairy Tales;
We were the rougher, restless ones—
'Snips and snails and puppy-dogs' tails';
Rugby for boys, netball for girls.
Learning to dance, you learned it backwards,
Following our manly lead, indeed!
How very much were you deceived;
How very much were we deceived.

Old courtesies came, passed down to us—
Giving up our seat on a bus,
Opening doors, ladies first.
We minded our language when ladies arrived;
Quaint old manners, in their dying days,
When gentlemen their caps would raise—
Surely never meant to patronise,
But hold in high esteem, and prize.
If we misjudged you, forgive us please:
How very much were we deceived.

Yet ladies, let it be admitted:
All our leadership, at length
Was founded on your female strength—
We, inclined to preen, and fight;
You, our purpose and our light—
Now revealing untapped talents
To give the world a fairer balance—
Scoring tries, claiming your rights,
Bearing arms, becoming our bosses—
However much we were deceived,
We hope that not too much is lost—
And may the gains outweigh the losses.

HERMAPHRODITES

Nature, it would seem, developed a plan—
To separate us, woman from man,
Such that to replicate our kind,
One must the other seek, and find;
And so as never to confuse,
Left us mortals various clues:

She's the smoother, busier one,
Inheriting the leading part;
She chats to people; knows what's going on,
Good at passing news around;
She's the one gives birth to babies.
Intuitively homeward bound,
Central is she, bosom of the earth;
Hers the substance, his the show;
Outer sails he, peripheral from birth.
He's the hairier one, with deeper voice;
For all his vain performing arts,
He must play supporting parts
With rather less to say.

And yet, and yet, confusion reigns:
Quite why woman, at the heart of life,
Should ever choose to emulate
The ways of her lazier, coarser mate,
Is anybody's guess.
Why the heroine's now a hero,
The hostess is our host,
The actress is an actor,
Is anybody's guess.
With hearty Charlotte known as Charley,
And feisty Freda's known as Fred,
It can come as no surprise
To be addressing them as "Guys"—
Comics are all comedians now;
Precious few comediennes—
We're all becoming cockerels now;
The farmyard's running out of hens.

We risk upsetting Nature's plan
To separate us, woman from man—
Merging as Hermaphrodites,
No need for one to seek the other:
Replicating, doubtless, still be done,
But not with nearly so much fun.

PERSONAL BEST

As good as your manners and your deeds may be,
Bethink they could be better;
And then, why stop at better,
When you can aim for your personal best?
This world will honour none so much,
As each and every one of us
Who aimed for our personal best.

Where performance may be measured,
The records honour the gifted few;
The brightest, the fastest, the strongest,
Caught up in such a limited quest,
Simply in finishing first,
Being better than all the rest.

But posterity values on a different scale,
The gold standard within each of us—
As many bests as there are people;
For all our flaws and limitations,
Personal bests encourage the rest—
We light each other's candles,
Examples we set and follow.
And following down the years
The good, the better, the best,
When we compete against ourselves,
We know when we've done our best.
And the world will honour none so much
As people who aimed for their personal best.

ANGEL

Can there be anything less angelic,
Than the Angel of the North?
Ill-conceived, misbegotten,
Inside some ballooning ego—
Some in-breeding of the human kind,
Drained of all humility, taste—
To whom this natural world of ours
Lies sickly short, of what it should be,
Desperate for our healing fingers:
Stillborn, of course, frozen stiff,
Gaunt with rectilinear wings,
Utterly lifeless, stark and flightless.

How much kinder it would have been,
Discreetly, to melt it down,
Instead of impaling it up there,
Like some mocking crucifixion—
To what purpose, may we despair—
Naked, in its Emperor's clothes,
Presuming to surmount the hills,
Usurp the very sky itself;
Effrontery made manifest,
Insulting to both Heaven and Earth.
If this be an Angel,
May we never meet the Lord it serves.

SUN DISCIPLES

In the sweltering heights of summer,
If you see us out and about, at all,
It'll be on the shady side of the street,
In some covered way, or shopping mall.

We are the blond, the ginger, the fair,
With light blue eyes and sensitive skin.

More likely we'll be staying in,
Sheltering in the coolest places,
Or following the shadows round the house
With wide-brimmed hat and pinking faces.

We are the blond, the ginger, the fair,
With light blue eyes and sensitive skin.

Oh, you tanned and handsome devotees,
Semi-naked sun disciples,
Exhibiting, all summer through,
Tobacco-toned heroic features
Along the promenades and beaches—
I suppose you think we envy you.

All right, I suppose, in a way, we do;
No use pretending, we just do.

But, it takes all types, you know:
What if we were all the same, like you—
No one blond, or ginger, or fair;
Everyone leathery, and tanned;
No light blue eyes or sensitive skin;
No one to make you look so proud—
How could you stand out from the crowd?

This, of course, is our hidden purpose;
Ours is such a higher calling—
We sensitive souls with light blue eyes,
Morale-uplifters in disguise—
Conspicuously without a tan,
Here to look much browner than.

LEA BAILEY

In ancient folklore, it is told,
This rough, ungoverned wilderness,
Between the Severn and the Wye,
Caught the ever-watchful eye
Of our wise, benevolent Woodland Queen,
Who gathered us under her woodland wings,
Declaring us Royal Forest of Dean.

Our damp and shadowy northern corner,
With all its handy draining waters,
She favoured as her private quarters—
A haven from the public gaze,
Where the forest may relieve itself
Discreetly, on the Queen's behalf—
As well becomes a Queen.

One end she dubbed a Brook Dry end,
The other of course a Watery end;
In between, the "Forest Drainage",
Along the length of which, uncoiled
The ribbon of Lea Bailey Lane,
As well for travellers passing through
As form a tidy bias binding,
To keep the forest skirt from fraying,
Doing what she has to do.

Then to appoint a Privy Council,
Keepers of the Privy Drainage—
The most dependable of neighbours,

Women and men as good as their words,
Whose every instinct is to help,
Loyal subjects all, of yeoman stock—
Bailiffs of her private quarters,
In various rustic domiciles,
Along our Bailiwick of Lea.
No serfdom this, but valued service,
For as loyal as we, to our Woodland Queen,
So in return, loyal is she.

Ancient folklore is no fable,
For many truths are so enshrined
In understandings of mankind.
Wandering through her paths and trails,
Opening minds to her listening trees,
We never fail to feel her welcome,
And something motherly in her care—
Her lessons there for us to learn,
As once, upon our mothers' knees.

And with her ever-watchful eye,
In ever-grateful supervision,
Day and night, dusk and dawn,
Her buzzards through the daylight hours,
The night-shift of her tawny-owls,
Her woodland courtiers overfly
The Privy Drainage and its Keepers—
Keeping the Keepers safe and well
Who serve their benevolent Woodland Queen,
Here in the Royal Forest of Dean.

SCULPTURE TRAILS

If we are going to have forests,
And of course we must,
Let us have forests worthy of the name—
Set apart from coppicing and logging —
Forests we keep our human hands off:
Forests to resuscitate the Earth,
To flourish and spread in Nature's way,
Free to be a wilderness,
And mercifully free from sculpture trails,
Oh, blissfully free from sculpture trails.

Why else explore a forest,
But partake, as it were, of the trees—
Sycamore, oak, hornbeam, beech;
Birch, hazel, chestnut, pine—
Their seasonal variations,
Their bark, and shapes of leaves,
Their shade, their fruit, their sounds;
Their very presence, character, age,
And the teeming life they harbour:
If you can get bored with these,
You are very hard to please.

Why else explore a forest,
But listen and watch for woodpeckers, jays,
Nuthatches, pigeons and warblers,
Owls, buzzards, tits and finches?
Watch for squirrels, deer, stoats and voles—
If you can get bored with these,
You are so very hard to please.

Why else explore a forest,
But what is there, for you to witness,
To glimpse and be aware of there—
Beetles, spiders, snails,
Dragonflies, moths, butterflies?
To step by snowdrops, wood anemone,
Primrose, ivy, orchids, bluebells,
And the multiform family of fungi:
If you can get bored with all these,
You are quite impossible to please.

There is no 'natural setting' for works of art:
Whatever we perceive them to be—
Ingenious, eloquent, inspiring,
Or such pretentious tripe,

Sculptures are artefacts, by definition;
Artificial; works of art,
Fabrications, by woman and man.
Their appropriate setting, surely,
Town square, campus, galleries,
Built environment of modern man,
Not in the depths of a forest.

Let us leave our woodlands, our forests,
Whatever remains of our natural world,
In something like its natural state:
So much more interest here,
Much, much more enlightenment here,
Than a hundred sculpture trails.
Nature trails, by all means,
But away with wretched sculpture trails.

BEAUTIFUL GAME

May we have our ball back, Mister?
Our Football back— Saturday Afternoons.
It was our National Sport, you know:
With few exceptions, all matches
Were on Saturday Afternoons,
And with few exceptions, all players,
All Managers, in the English Leagues
Were English, or British—
And with few exceptions, games were played
Within a conscious Code of Conduct.

May we have our ball back, Mister?
English Leagues are not very English now:
Sometimes, in a starting eleven,
There are no English at all.
And so it is, in international tournaments,
Many of our top League players
Line up against our National side,
Depleting and defeating us;
Nor very surprising to find
Foreigners managing the England Team.

May we have our ball back, Mister?
Club after Club has sold its soul
To television companies:
Football is for Saturday Afternoons,
Not weekday evenings, under floodlights.
How depressing it all is, to see
Our National game awash with money,
And millionaire players ten-a-penny—
Clubs able and willing to pay them
Several years' wages, every week.

May we have our ball back, Mister?
And may we have sportsmanship, discipline,
Dignity, good conduct back again?
Give us back respect for our game:
No more juvenile petulance,
No more 'diving' or 'professional fouls',
No more 'mobbing' of the Referee,
No more mouthing of obscenities,
No more spitting, disgusting nostril-snorting,
Nor shaking the head in disbelief.
Wasn't that a deliberate foul?
No, just 'taking one for the team'.

May we have our ball back, Mister?
Quite unaware of itself, and blind
To its ironies, the professional game
Drifts off in a vast bubble of vanity,
Puffing itself up, glamourising:
Surely League Number One is the top?
Good Heavens no! There's Championship,
Premiership, higher than that;
Stand by for Super, Ultimate leagues:
Linesmen are 'Assistant Referees',
Managers have their 'Technical Areas';
No forwards now, but 'Strikers'
It's not your first game for the team,
It is your public 'Debut'!
Players are 'Icons', 'Legends', no less;
Goals in extra-time are
'Sudden Death' goals, no less.

May we have our ball back, Mister?
A goal scored arises from sound defence,
Skilful approach play, incisive
Passing and crossing of the ball—
Yet the Striker who taps it in

Cavorts in an ecstasy of
Self-adoration and glory—
Seemingly unaware that all he did
Was to score another goal
In another football match.

May we have our Football back, please?
Our National Sport should be a living
Example to us all, of honest endeavour,
Living and playing within the Rules—
Where goalkeepers, knowing the ball, unnoticed,
Has crossed their line, run to tell the Referee—
Instead of following fake glory,
Follow the morality, play the game.
Let us bring no more shame
To what should be our Beautiful Game.

INTELLIGENCE

Whatsoever that Vast Loom, whereon
Our universe is spun,
It seems so lacking of a purpose,
That some such beneficial purpose
Has to be imputed—
For anything, anything, to make sense
To those of us, of heart and eye,
Who gaze up to our evening sky,
Feeling the need to measure ourselves,
Assess ourselves, against such
Vague and hopeful observations and,
Self-conscious creatures that we are,
Imagine a universe gazing back—
How we are regarded, from afar.

Randomly, in every Epoch,
Interstellar briefings are released;
A universal Taking Stock:
And this latest, we can scarce avoid—
For all Galactic Observations,
From comets, moons and asteroids,
Point to our local Solar System
And planet Helios Number Three:

"Within her fecund and prodigious waters,
Multifarious forms have spawned", they say,
"Born to replicate themselves, for ever,
Born but to die, in numbers
Countless, that one must thrive
At the cost of another, and many,
Countless more, have crawled", they say,
"From those waters on to land,
To the plains, the hills, the trees—

"And one particular form of these,
One astonishing form of these,
Has drawn attention to itself, —
Across the vastnesses of space—
By all its cleverness, ingenuity,
Its arrogance, its fears and superstitions,
Entitlement, ownership and power,
Its wonderful creativity,
Restlessness but recklessness,
Its very own provenance, apparently
Disowned: Nature is here but
To be improved, refined.

"An inclination to destroy, not only
The very land it feeds upon, but
Turning against its own kind,
Prolifically killing its very own kind,
A kind of madness in the mind—
And such an overweening pride,
Not so much in parentage, but pedigree,
And philosophical aimlessness", they say,
"Blind, relentless questing, as if
There really is a Rainbow's End".

If you can see some grains of truth
In those interstellar briefings,
I can't help but agree:
One wonders exactly who it is
Who's lacking of a purpose,
And how we might redeem ourselves—
That should we ever venture into space,
We may expect a cordial welcome.

CARTOGRAPHY

We are naturally good at making maps,
So making maps is what we do,
Representing miles by inches—
And shrinking the world in this way
Is to magnify ourselves, a trend
Which feeds upon itself, through
Atlases and mounted Globes,
Affecting such a lofty eye
With a vantage point, here on high—
Assuming, as of birthright,
Inheritance, title and power,
All through our human knowledge:
And upon this tide of knowledge
We drift, afloat, from the Natural Order.

For all our microscopes and telescopes,
We are forced to admit, those we call
Lower Orders of Life, wherever they
Swim, crawl or fly, do not
Noticeably suffer, from a
Dearth of maps, or knowledge,
Nor presume to inherit the Earth—
Yet knowledge it is, with which we
Refine and garland ourselves—
Though it benefits no-one but
Ourselves, though it becomes
An End in itself, or a stairway somewhere higher:
If a stairway, let it show the way to Wisdom.

SHIP OF STATE

"What's a ship for," says the Gunner,
"If it's not to carry the weapons around?"
And of course he has a point.
"Well how will we know which way to steer,"
The Navigator adds,
"Without me plotting our course?"
"Fair point," notes the Chief,
"But the ship'll be staying right here,
If I don't flash up the boilers."
"And what if the telecoms fail,"
Says Sparks, "when we're way out at sea?"
And has a good point, of course.
At which the Catering Officer speaks —
"You gunners, plotters, oilers and sparkers,
How long will we last, do you think,
With nothing to eat or to drink?"

And so it is, with our Ship of State,
HMS United Kingdom—
Paddy and Tommy, Taffy and Jock,
One purpose, interdependently,
When this fine warship puts to sea.

When this fine warship puts to sea,
Its overriding common cause
The best from every sailor draws …

... Spud Murphy, Pedlar Palmer, Dinger Bell,
Flash Gordon, Pincher Martin, Nobby Clarke,
Bungy Williams, Hooky Walker, Swampy Marsh,
Dusty Miller, Buster Brown, Sharky Ward ...

One crew there is, one crew on board;
From what shires, from whichever towns—
Geordies or Scousers or Brummies,
Oggies, Cockneys, Moonrakers, Hampshire Hogs;
Whichever accent, dialect, place of birth,
With this Ship's Company mustered,
In HMS United Kingdom,
I doubt you'll find a finer crew on Earth.

CENOTAPH

Hard to think of a nobler cause,
Calling for binding comradeship;
Hard to think of comradeship
In pursuit of a nobler cause
Than the safety of our people,
And the freedom of our land.

And so we gather along Whitehall,
Or witness, from our homes,
As if summoned by the Fallen—
Nor need we a second bidding:
Armistice Day, the Cenotaph, empty tomb,
Everlasting strength and fellowship,
Expressed in Portland Stone.

Undiminished through the years,
Intuitive, known and choreographed—
What can we, but give way
To our High Priestess, Ceremony,
And her sacraments though the Day?

Were we the Fallen, they'd have done the same,
We just know it, can't help but show it;
Its essence lies in comradeship,
And such a welling sureness, and a pride,
That we are on the right and honourable side.

PROPOSAL

Don't misunderstand me, Mary—
Let me not equivocate,
Let me never be contrary,
But casting off my doubts,
Holding back no longer, my dear,
My aspirations to make clear.

Don't misunderstand me, Mary—
Never have I felt indifferent to you;
Far be it from me to say
You are not the prettiest of maids;
I'd fall well short of a suitor's duty,
If I failed to comment on your beauty.

Don't misunderstand me, Mary—
I will not deny the public rumour
About your rustic sense of humour;
Nor am I disinclined to laugh,
For the cow-shed humour of the farm
Can never undermine your charm.

Don't misunderstand me, Mary—
What earthly good would books have been
Against your native intuition?
And would I dare to challenge your views?
My arguments would be in vain
Against your clear, uncluttered brain.

Don't misunderstand me, Mary—
With star-signs mystically aligned,
And the way you bluntly speak your mind,
I wouldn't say we're badly matched—
And, not wishing to avoid the truth,
We're both beyond the budding of youth.

Don't misunderstand me, Mary—
T'is to your heart that I lay claim,
Now that you have lit my flame.
I feel that fate is beckoning us—
Cupid aims his bow at us,
And trusting that his aim is true,
Who would rate our prospects gloomy,
Were I at last to draw you to me?

PROPHECY

I dare say the racial problem
Is bigger than all of us, put together.
I almost dare not say it,
But if I don't I'll wish I had:
All of us, placed together by law,
By direction from on high,
By culture, by type or inclination,
Eventually will cleave
To fellow cultural groupings
Within the artificial whole—
Pretending to a uniformity
Which so lacks cohesion.

Sooner or later, it will dawn on us;
It has already dawned, I dare say,
Privately on most of us,
But public admission, sooner or later,
Will have to be made, and faced—
The General Multicultural Delusion
Will have to be confessed.

And we must sincerely hope,
That the inevitable partitioning
Can be realised by Treaties,
Before it is forced upon us
By much less peaceful means.

There is no assessing of human nature
By rosy wishful thinking;
We have to consult raw feelings,
Consult our primary feelings,
And trust them before our schooling
And our intellect; listen more to
What might be called our hearts,
Than to academic orthodoxies.
We are by nature who we are,
Not what priests or politicians
Like to imagine us to be.
Someone has to dare to say so.

ADJACENT SEAT

I had simply lacked the courage
To go and sit beside her,
When there was an adjacent seat:
How wonderful she could feel so free
To come, unbidden, to sit by me—
With such gentleness in her voice,
And such honesty in her eyes.

There were several other vacant seats,
But she came to sit by me,
If, please, I would not mind;
Indeed, indeed, I did not mind.
Made her feel more secure, said she,
With gentleness in her voice,
And honesty in her eyes.

She did not know me, but
She had seen me there before;
I did not know her, but
I had seen her there before,
And sensed a certain confident charm
In that unknown lady I saw.
Whenever there is, I asked, an adjacent seat,
Might I come to sit beside her
If, please, she would not mind?
She would not mind, said she;
It would make her feel secure, said she,
With gentleness in her voice,
And honesty in her eyes.

And on the very next occasion,
There was an adjacent seat,
So I went to sit beside her.
And indeed she did not mind.
I hoped she had been saving it for me.
It made her feel secure, said she,
With gentleness in her voice,
And honesty in her eyes.

When I offered her my address,
She answered, simply, yes,
With gentleness in her voice,
And honesty in her eyes.
And then, when I wondered where she lived,
(Somewhere near Heaven, was my guess)
She gave it gladly; gave it gladly, yes!
With gentleness in her voice,
And honesty in her eyes,
This utterly lovely lady
Wrote down for me her home address.

CLAPPING

Now we are up and balanced, on our hindmost feet,
Our front pair - let us call them 'hands'—
Are free to grasp, grab, gesticulate,
To beat our chests, scratch and punch,
With fingers to point out, and they're
Good for grooming and caressing—
And for slapping together as a signal
Or for scaring other creatures off—
Sharp, percussive sound, which we
Might call an onomatopoeic 'clap':
Who would have thought that as time went by,
Percussive slaps of our two front paws,
Would constitute a round of applause?

Unimaginable, of course, that we could
Ever be so organised, so cultured and
So civilised, to act collectively,
Responding rapturously, to a concert
Of music or performing arts.

And only together, communally,
Does clapping meet our needs—
A handy adaptation, we might call it—
Of a bonding, herding instinct;
It is collective, or it is nothing.
Let one person only, begin to clap:
Within four seconds will he cease,
Unless several others follow, and
His blushes are saved in general applause.

He will not be so forward again—
Quite unthinkable, in a packed and
Orderly House, is clapping solo.

Mostly below the threshold of cheering, calling,
Clapping is appreciation in restraint,
With nuances, nevertheless;
Applause can be noticeably polite,
Or vigorous, fulsome and sustained,
Topped up with calls for more;
Or receive a rhythmic slow hand-clap,
And you'll never forget that day.

It seems so very natural now,
Deploying our handiest means of all
For communal expression,
And within its bare simplicity
There is poignancy, and refinement:
Amongst the thousands, from the terraces,
We roar our teams to victory—
But fall silent, when a player is
Badly injured— and when the poor fellow
Is stretchered off, instinctively, respectfully, we clap.

TACTILE

Dear Tactile, Own House and Car,
Seeking Companionship, Maybe More—

Do let me be the one you seek,
A kindred spirit, it would seem,
Searching for you near and far;
Waiting for you, rich or poor—
Companionship, and maybe more.

Dear Tactile, Own House and Car—
Yes! books and learning, history, the arts,
Looking things up and finding things out,
Comprehending who we are—
A world of interest we'd explore,
Companionship, and maybe more.

Dear Tactile, Own House and Car—
Yes! country rambles, country pubs,
Log fires and ploughman's lunches,
Simple inexpensive pleasures—
Between us how we could restore
Companionship, and maybe more.

Oh, Touchable Tactile, whoever you are,
With or without your house and car,
Do, please, shine your light on me,
And do be pleased with what you see:
Reach and touch my outstretched hand,
And let there flow between us
All that makes for peace of mind,
Sharing the truth and being kind—
And may it last for evermore,
Companionship and so much more.

DEEP SLEEP

If we could howl completely, as a baby howls,
Emptying, wringing out our souls,
Then might we sleep as a baby sleeps—
Collapsing in a carefree coma,
Vulnerable and unaware,
Unselfconscious, utterly elsewhere;
Waking up without a care
For what transpired while we were there.

But being burdened, tried and tested,
We know too much to be purged of such,
No matter how we weep.
And when we do get a good night's sleep,
The clocks keep vigil, and verify
That several hours have drifted by—
But we know them never:
As if by Time just left behind
With the fairies and the babies,
To be collected by and by.

But what of those baby-sleeping hours?
To anticipate, but never know,
Just where all the saints and babies go?
Such a blessed therapy is sleep—
Reveries, meandering free,
Minds that so need pottering times,
Pottering about their secret gardens—
And we can never know
What seeds there may be sown,
What slugs and snails therein slain;
For such therapy who would not howl,
That we might sleep as a baby sleeps?
Lived, but lost beyond recall,
Deep sleep as a hope of Heaven on Earth.

CASTING VOTE

There may be times when we can't agree,
So we really must decide,
Before we actually 'tie the knot',
Who will have the casting vote,
Who will have the final say—
And I guess, it should be me.

Sometimes we're bound to disagree,
But if you really loved me,
You'd want me to have my way—
It were best be me, with the final say.

Well I could say the very same,
That it might as well be me;
I might well claim, being the elder,
The honour naturally falls to me.

We could have topics allocated—
You decide on some things; I decide on others—
But you would want the bigger ones,
And leave the trivial ones for me.

We might as well take turns—
Be leader on alternate days—
But then we'd never have discussions,
Except on one of your days.

Look, should we really need a casting vote?
We're surely grown-up enough
To do without this final-saying stuff;
We can simply talk things through,
Put our personal points of view,
As sensible, grown-up people do.

Yes, of course, talk through and through,
But if we still cannot agree?
If what suits you does not suit me?
Surely one must have the final say.

But, my dear, do you not see—
Happiness is equality:
Nobody leading, nobody following—
Freedom to be ourselves,
In individuality.

So, if you say left and I say right,
We take the middle way;
If you say black and I say white,
Then all we have is grey—
Something tells me that, between us,
We've just been having the final say:
I guess we've decided, whether or not
To go ahead, and tie this knot.

OPTING OUT

When someone shakes a collecting-tin,
In the name of some popular cause,
Just smile if you like, and pass on by—
The opting out is always yours.
When a show of hands in a Lecture Hall,
Confirms the speaker's point of view,
I always admire the dissenting few
Who will not be cowed by his challenge.

'To opt', being to exercise a
Personal choice, I'd like to see
Less of, indeed the end of,
All official assumptions
That I have exercised a choice,
When I have not.
Such assumptions take a moralistic
Stance, which may not be mine—
Seeming to dare me to reveal
A less honourable point of view
Than theirs: That very assumption
Is dishonourable, it seems to me,
Running counter to the ethos
Of a free and democratic people.

And morality, moreover, often
Is subjective, far from self-evident;
Official assumptions have no place here:
No shame nor blame must attach
To minority points of view;
This is the beauty of the secret ballot,
Removing every chance of
Intimidation and embarrassment.

And so, to incorporate, in official documents,
An angelic point of view—
That upon our demise, we all
Wish to donate our organs
Is reprehensible— inviting us
To reveal ourselves as callous and inhuman.

We must never shrink from opting out,
If that is how we feel.

DEAD RECKONING

What Ship? Where Bound?
Far out at sea, keeping watch by night;
Overcast, no guiding stars,
Devoid of compass bearings,
Dead-reckoning through the dark—
With sea-born, oceanic thoughts
Drifting beyond horizons—
Estimating Latitudes and Longitudes,
An old interrogating voice intrudes:
What Ship? Where Bound?

How on Earth are we supposed to know—
Devoid of compass bearings—
Dead-reckoning through the dark?
Part of some great purpose, are we?
Or stranded, up on evolution's beach?
Born to serve, dying to know?
Let us all be thankful that
The answers lie beyond our reach.

What Ship? Where Bound?
What course might we plot, if all were known,
Truth and purpose all foretold?
What earthly use for us to know?
Where would hope and wonder go?
Better far, this quest, where we may ponder
What may be yonder, what may befall—
Far out at sea, keeping watch by night,
Dead-reckoning through the dark:
Sea-farers need their seas.

What Ship? Where Bound?
My guess is, we are safe and sound—
For sooner will a housefly explain,
How it is thwarted by a window pane.

ELBOW LANE

I'm not sure where it was—
In the West Country somewhere, I recall,
Oh, forty years or more ago, but
What did lodge in my mind was
That sign— 'Formerly Elbow Lane'.

Strolling down a busy street, I
Caught sight of it, as I crossed
The entrance to a narrow alley
To my right. So taken was I
By the former name, that I have
No recall at all, of its new,
'Improved' name, fastened just above it.
That charming former name has lingered
In my mind ever since – with a
Wonder why it could not stay.

As a kind of irony, there beneath the
Later name, it was the more conspicuous—
A twinge of conscience, it would seem,
At futility in such changes,
Even a kind of guilt.
Without any understanding, but
Such an abiding interest, in such
Revised thinking, I fail to imagine
The proceedings of that revising Council,
Which endorsed this bright proposal,
And several others like it, no doubt.

But I like to imagine a brave old
Councillor, with English blood in his veins,
And West Country mud on his boots,
Taking a stand, wringing this concession
From the Council's Business in Hand
Of re-naming the ancient alley way—
Reminding passers-by in future years,
That it was 'Formerly Elbow Lane'.

WHO'S WHO

Well no, we don't know who you are.
But, whoever you may be—
Of some consequence, it seems,
By wealth, or office, or birth—
Presuming to inherit the Earth,
And that we should know of you,
And seemingly be in awe of you.

No, we don't know who you are.
But, why keep us guessing?
Whoever you are, you'll have our blessing—
Majestic or Regal or Holy—
If you're modest, and courteous, and kind.
Why should it matter to us?
Why ever should we mind?

But, no need to tell us now;
We already know enough.
We will Obey, if obedience is due,
But Respect is of a different hue—
And any respect that may be due
Calls for a different tone of voice,
For hearts and minds to follow through.

So, asking if we know who you are
May not get you very far:
May we introduce our selves, and
May we, as equals, put to you,
Humanity's nought to do with rank—
We all have credit in the Human Bank—
We are the citizens, the taxpayers, the voters:
No more, no less, than you, are we;
No more, no less, and ever will be.

INEVITABILITY

Some countries in the world are known as 'Free'—
Known as such by virtue of a premise
That the people, all the people, effectively
Run their country. By general franchise,
Regular elections, free and fair,
With secret ballots and a wide choice
Of political parties – and by freedom
Of the press, print and broadcast,
The people are free. Politicians,
Always, are answerable to the people.
The same philosophy implies a
Transparent judicial system, with
Equal access to healthcare, education
And employment, in a market
Economy of free enterprise.

Other countries there are, with very few
Such liberties, with fraudulent elections,
If any at all, and bogus results
Announced as outright endorsement
Of the leaders. The people are answerable
To the leaders, who prefer to be
Feared, rather than respected.

This philosophy implies a
Strictly government-controlled press,
Corrupt judicial system, repression
And removal of dissenters, preferential
Treatment of the ruling elite, behind
A mask of fairness and democracy.

Anything more need hardly be said,
But it must be said, in the name of
Justifying hope, and the general morale
Of the people of the world:
For however long it takes, one day,
One Day, all peoples will be free.

It cannot be otherwise, for whatever
Setbacks may intervene, whatever gains
By political or religious fanatics,
There can be no doubt that person by
Person, town by town, country by country,
Increment by frustrating increment,
People are bound to opt for freedom.

Much more than probable, we can say:
It is the only possible way.

TONGUE

You don't need me to tell you, but
When you enjoy a hearty meal, there's
No need for you to think about it,
To think about the eating of it:
Think about anything on your mind,
Or chat to the person next to you;
If anything is amiss, your old
Dependable tongue will soon let you know.

With a provenance hopelessly lost
In Time, your versatile tongue,
Incomparably flexible, is Matron
Of the Mouthparts, gums and
Teeth, palates hard and soft,
Supervisor in saliva:
Autonomous too, having no need for you—
Whatever you have on your mind—
Simply relies on your instinct to chew.

That's all she needs, and all
She has ever needed, to take from
Your fingers the food you choose,
Assign it to available teeth,
And without a conscious thought from you,
Follow the rhythm of ages,
Synchronising every munch,
Distributing food, avoiding teeth,
Shifting food, avoiding teeth,
Changing sides, preparing a mash,
Rejecting indigestible bits,

Rolling a suitable bolus of pulp,
Fit for the fundamental swallow.
And without prompting, each course
Swallowed, she inspects the ranks of
Teeth for bits being trapped,
Probing and dislodging them, or
Letting you know if she can't.

And should you be a talkative eater
She will, without prior notice,
Articulate and shape each and
Every word for you, switching

From Matron to eloquent servant, and back
At the drop of a conversational thought;
Dissimilar duties though they be,
She recollects – I know not how—
All your consonants, all your vowels.

Say what you like about the heart,
It's the tongue that takes some beating:
Do you say you speak from the heart?
My guess would be, the tongue—
And what has your heart ever done
To help you with your eating?
Or licking your lips? Or spitting out pips?
Is English language known as a Heart?
No, it's known as a Tongue.

Matron of our Mouthparts,
Our Tasting and our Talking,
Anatomical Superstar,
Out of sight and out of mind,
Whose accomplices we surely are.

THIS LANGUAGE

This language we have today,
It took a long time to get here:
From "First Light" of our human dawn,
When ideas slowly struggled free,
And minds gave birth to words—
Or words, perhaps, to minds—
Resolving what was ill-defined
To number or shape, location or kind,
To modern conversation, to our songs,
To this language we have today.

Alas, this language we have today,
For all the time it's taken,
Has somehow grown along the way
Carbuncles on our speech—
B-words, S-words, C-words, F-words—
As if to fill some verbal voids—
Echoes of primordial screech
Whereto our language cannot reach,
Even as primeval howls
Must have shaped our modern vowels.

Dropped your car-keys down the drain?
'Dearie-me' won't take the strain;
Jammed your fingers in the gate?
'Golly-gosh' won't compensate;

Dropped your i-phone down the loo?
Lost your passport in Peru?
Stepped in a smelly pile of poo?
'Oh how tiresome' will not do.

There may be circumstances, then,
In this language we have today,
For want of cultured substitutes
When only primitive words will fit.

We'd better learn to live with them,
As something wild that can't be tamed—
And maybe graciously admit
They simply will not go away,
But may adorn, as well contaminate,
This language we have today.

COFFEE SHOP

If I'm early enough, to the coffee shop,
I get my favourite window seat
With a window view, out to the street,
And sip in silent observation,
Casting my infallible eye
On unsuspecting passers-by.
But if I should arrive too late,
I have to make do with an inside seat,
And then I have to concentrate—
Sipping in silent observation,
Casting my infallible eye
A little more discreetly.
And more than idle speculation,
Each sipping simply verifies:—

Those two, chalk and cheese, to my eyes;
I don't know what she sees in him—
She does seem rather old for him—

No wonder that one's on her own;
All tattoos and gaudy shoes
I could never come in looking like that—

Clearly here she's on display,
Coffee-watching all the others,
But catch her eye, she'll look away—

And the usual push-chair couple
Attending to each other no more
Than they do to the child,
Fancy bringing a toddler in anyway—

Like that tired old fellow yonder,
Some problem at home, I shouldn't wonder—
Always here when I come in;
Nothing better to do, it seems—

And the foreign-looking two back there,
More than just friends, I bet, that pair;
Never seems to wash her hair,
Some people just can't be bothered.

Incontrovertible until, draining my cup,
I make my way to the street,
And idling past the window-fronts,
For some reason, I look up:
To that unflattering image of myself—
Contemplating my disguise
Before the world's infallible eyes,
And once again, am I reminded
How often are we so blinded
By whatever only eyes can see.

AM and PM

By no means to diminish the importance
Of viruses which threaten our health,
And even endanger our lives,
Let us also be aware of
Social viruses, threatening not our health,
But insidious none the less.

Residents around here received a letter,
A helpful and informative letter,
About closure of roads for maintenance:
These closures would be necessary, it said,
Between 09.00 hours and 17.00 hours.

I don't know about you (Well,
In this respect I'm sure I do), but
I've never heard people here at home,
In our gardens or in our streets,
Talk in such affected terms.
They will say, we will say, you will say
"They'll be closed from Nine o'clock to Five"
It seems to be a legacy of
Being in the European Union—
But now we are free, what
Possible purpose can be served
By this pompous affectation,
Which lingers like a virus
Within our daily lives?

The twenty-four hour clock has its place
Of course, in military matters,
And I guess, in international travel,
But it surely has no place around here.

Sadly, some of our indigenous folk
Succumb to the affectation virus:
A country pub I drove past
A year or two ago, advertised
A skittles match, not for 8.00 pm
But for 20.00 hours.
"Twenty Hundred Hours"—
A skittles match, in an English country pub.

HUMAN RESOURCES

To think of the years we wretches have toiled,
Knowing not what we were doing,
Nor on whose behalf; no sense of purpose
But emptiness and confusion:
What were we to make of those two opaque,
Impenetrable words— 'Personnel' and 'Department'
Clogging up the nation's industries?
Words bewildering us all, no matter
How many times we looked them up—
"That part of a Company that deals with
Appointment, welfare and records of employees"—
What unfathomable, obfuscating Gobbledegook!

But now, great mercy and thanks to Heaven,
Or one of Heaven's Delegates on Earth,
Now are we delivered from darkness,
Now the bright sunlit uplands beckon—
Great, Liberating, Clarifying Rainbow—
At long, long last we find that
People who work here are Human Resources:
To the Almighty, Glory Be!
We are all Resources, of the human kind.

WEDLOCK

Little resembling deer or feathered fowl,
On Wedding Eve we are stags and hens:
'Man-night', 'Woman night' will not do;
We bellow as stags, squawk as hens—
Rituals to make one wonder,
Venturing in from the wild,
How much we hail a beginning,
How much lament an end.

For on the morrow, we'll be authorised—
Ringed, recorded and sworn,
Tidied up as bride and groom,
To make common cause with customs and laws:
Bound in Holy Wedlock.

Odd, unlikely words, stag and hen,
Instead of calling us women and men—
As odd as calling us bride and groom:
Could it be we borrow their names,
As serving to mark and emphasise
A certain art and artifice
In procedures matrimonial,
For wanderers in from the wild,
Binding a nature that will not be bound,
As if to remind us of who we are,
While losing sight of what we are?

PREROGATIVE

Born in Nineteen Thirty-seven,
I am a child of my Time,
For better or for worse,
As English as can be—
A somewhat inertial thing
In an ever-shifting world,
Clinging to custom and tradition,
As to a life-raft, as to what
Is familiar, and just seems right—
Acknowledging change and progress
Somewhat grudgingly, wistfully.

I was raised in the days when
Manhood meant entitlement,
Leadership, ownership and
Even superior wisdom, the falsity
And unlearning of which assumptions,
Have been uncomfortable, to say the least.

Sweeping statements are risky, of course,
For better or for worse,
But for guiding, homespun wisdom,
We must turn to the female senses:
An ancient resilience, it seems,
Inhabits the female temperament—
Intuitive, social antennae, quite beyond ours.

Understandably then, is the state
Of marriage, for better or for worse,
Called 'Matrimony', as if to acknowledge
Womanhood, motherhood,
The very nurturing at its core.

'Patrimony', be it noted, merely
Refers to estate, inheritance,
Matters legal and external.

In which context, clearly now I see,
One inherited custom, to which I clung,
Should support our society no more:
How misplaced, for a woman to
Have to wait and wonder if
Any man will propose.
It is not sufficient, that she may decline;
The initiative must be hers.

Destined to be the very heart of
Her marriage and family, her
Judgement will be at least as true,
Her criteria probably more cautious,
Broader and safer. Let proposing be
The Female Prerogative, for better
Or for worse, probably for better.

PRINCE PHILIP'S FUNERAL

It was not the signs, themselves,
That summoned forth our tears,
Nor those military disciplines,
But what they've come to represent—
A language, in salutes and gestures,
An outward show of what is rooted
Deep below, sub-conscious dread
It seems, at dimming of a guiding light;
Loss of landmark, compass bearing.

When first we heard the dreadful news,
I doubt we hardly shed a tear
'Til when, in public was it dramatised
In ceremonial procedures,
To mourn one local, earthly exemplar,
A kind of human guiding star.

For Pathfinders have we need, Leaders
Who seem to know and show the way,
Whose compasses know True North,
For us to trust, respect and follow—
And such was he, for all his eminence
A man of the people, of our Queen,
The Queen he respectfully walked behind:
Whichever faiths he was guided by,
Surely his overriding light
Was his faith in human kind.

LAUGHTER

Helping us get by, and cope—
When politeness is demanded,
A feeling needs disguising,
Or ingratiating fits the moment—
Like to a practised autograph,
Is the ever-ready pre-formed laugh:
"You'll laugh when I tell you this," they'll say:
We ready ourselves a pre-formed laugh.

But that which it affects to be—
That wild, inarticulate thing
Of the nerves, and inhibitions—
Involuntary spasms, which
Shake the very truth from us —
What outpouring joy it can be,
Helplessly liberating,
Helplessly bubbling free

But spontaneous laughter,
Just as soon as free us, may betray us
Well beyond affectation's reach.
A brief, spontaneous sample of the soul,
A momentary truth, sweet or sour—
When some word, or joke, or circumstance
Clicks a shutter, for an utterance's
Unexpected flight, a burst, a snort,
As soon again restrained, confined—
Just too late to keep hidden away,
For people who have thoughts to hide,
The depth of their demeanour, day by day.

CAMERA

Whence this sorcery in a camera lens
That so entrances Homo Sapiens?

When you are presented with your Winner's Cup,
Unless you urgently need to, do not kiss it, please;
And you, with your Winner's Gold Medal,
Do not bite it, please—
I can't stand it any more:
They are trophies, not placebo dummies;
You are champions, not performing seals;
Better to wait until you get home,
And spare us silly pictures in the papers.

Whence this sorcery in a camera lens
That so entrances Homo Sapiens?

If you pull a face in front of a camera,
You are either still at infants' school,
Or you've already sold your soul—
The lens has filleted your brains—
The camera has taken control:
Waiting for the button to be pressed,
You 'compose' yourself for the exposure,
With nothing half so much exposed
As your own wary, tense discomfort.

Whence this sorcery in a camera lens
That so entrances Homo Sapiens?

If we cannot be ourselves in front of it,
Just what is a camera?
And wherefore the spell it weaves?
I bet photographers work for God—
One way to keep an eye on us,
Wondering what we have to hide:
So we must look our Sunday Best,
Standing where we're placed, ready and braced,
Deep frozen for the family album.

Whence this sorcery in a camera lens
That so entrances Homo Sapiens?

Whatever it is we have to hide,
By impenetrable faces, carapaces,
I doubt we know ourselves—
But of earthly creatures, it would seem,
We only, conscious of ourselves—
And this is where a photographer delves:
It's time we sent them back to their Boss
To advise He focus more on Sinners,
Than embarrassing Cup and Medal Winners.

HOLDING HANDS

The customary greeting, face to face,
Is the clasp of two right hands;
Acquaintance acknowledged,
Thumbs together, on equal terms.
But with the well-acquainted, strolling side by side,
A joining of hands is right with left,
Not so obviously equal terms,
For one thumb only can prevail;
The other must appear to yield,
Implicitly agreed, on joining hands.
But this is no yielding, side by side,
No leader nor a led implied:
Protector and protected it may be,
But its essence is in unity.

Notions of leading and being led,
In our egalitarian age,
May be why couples go strolling free,
Keeping to themselves
In all their individuality;
Except a parent with a child,
No need for clasping hands.

Let's hope they soon grow up to see
That hands are joined in unity—
To make the incomplete complete,
Mutuality of hope and wish,
A dovetailing of minds.

For complementary needs and purposes
Do people hold each other's hands:
Not of rank, but of function and role,
A finding of what was missing,
With all the old familiar charm
Of lovers strolling arm-in-arm.

COVID CHRISTMAS 2020

With dark, pandemic clouds
Menacing mankind,
Coronavirus chills, and culls;
Bids us stay at home,
Wear facemasks, keep social distance,
But when it dares to threaten Christmas,
Great festival of hope and faith,
There'll be a turning of the tide—
Coronavirus on the losing side—
By simple goodness vanquished:
Communities, neighbours, fellowship,
By parishes and people.

"About our future meetings
Of Aston Ingham WI,
With masks and social distancing,
Janet will be in touch, by and by.
Please contact Hazel about
Coffee-mornings, lunches, whist-drives
And country-dancing in the Village Hall.
And following Church of England guidelines,
The church is open now for private prayer."

"Enjoy the Christmas Story at Upton Bishop:
At Bethlehem, see the Shepherds and Wise Men;
Meet Mary, Joseph, Baby Jesus at the stable,
Mince pies, mulled wine, all available.
Please book an arrival time,
To ensure social distancing."

"Wonderful start to the new school year
In Lea Primary and Pre-School,
Learning of the Great Fire of London,
Thanks to the parents of Willow Class.
But to walkers and dog-owners,
Be responsible, please—
Clear up, with your pooper-bags,
And no more discarded facemasks."

"Sweets and candles and oranges
At Linton Christingle service—
So what's not to like?
Contact Charlotte at Wrens' Nest
For how many seats you need:
Singing by choirs and soloists only,
And masks must be worn."

"The Fairies and Elves of Gorsley
Are filling hampers with goodies:
If you're a family needing help,
In this time of Covid,
Just let Sarah know."

EU TRADE TALKS, 2020

Between the two opposing sides
Was a Deadline solemnly agreed,
That would sharpen their discussion:
Without a settled date,
Minds might meander,
Not concentrating on the deal,
And best possible compromise.

But when that Deadline drew near,
Each side felt so close
To getting what they wished for—
And the other side might give way—
So postponed the 'Deadline' to another day.

When this second 'Deadline' drew near,
Each side felt so close
To getting what they wished for—
And the other side might give way—
So postponed this 'Deadline' to another day.
And yet again, until it was clear
How grotesquely misnamed
Was 'Deadline Day':
The 'Deadline' was no line,
But a smudge, a smear, a fudge;
It knew nothing about death,
Only life everlasting—
'Solemn Agreements' were no such thing,
But mutually insincere.

Each delegation, less to its purpose
Than to its pride, lost all thought
Of millions watching, or listening in,
Whose very enterprises, futures,
Fears and hopes were hanging
On that agreement being sealed.

The very device, The Deadline,
Established by convention, common sense
To focus, concentrate the minds—
Wantonly dishonoured,
The waiting public wantonly misused,
Our English language wantonly abused.

PASS IT ON

There's a rumour going round
That we've left the European Union—
Please pass it on.
There's rumour that we've reclaimed
Our British way of life at last—
Please pass it on.

There's a rumour going round
That everything is homeward bound—
That we're reinstating British laws,
Not subordinate to theirs,
But now to run our own affairs;
That we've taken back our borders,
And reclaimed our fishing grounds—
Do, please, pass it on.

And even rumours flying round,
That we're bringing back the pound—
The pound of weight, that is—
Along with hundredweights and ounces,
And tons spelt with a single 'n'—
Doing away with kilograms,
Never to let them in again.
Do, please, pass it on.

There's talk, among the rumour-makers
Of hectares coming back to acres.
What's more, it's even being said,
Liquid litres will be dead—
Pints and quarts and gallons instead.
Do, please, pass it on.

And, at last, those wretched metres
Will go the way of liquid litres—
Foreign measures giving way
To furlongs, yards and miles and all:
Things will be feet and inches long,
People feet and inches tall.
Everybody, pass it on.

From foreign measures long decreed,
By democratic voices freed:
How it will gladden native hearts,
To read familiar maps and charts—
The seas around us fathoms deep,
Temperatures in Fahrenheit,
Mountains not of metres, but of feet.
Everybody, pass it on.

And so, to politicians: please—
Our servants be, and not our masters.
You really must at last concede,
Respecting democratic creed—
If you ask us voters what we want,
The reply we give, is what we want;
No more telling us what we need.
All the rumours going round—
You may assume them to be true,
All by democratic process bound;
You, accountable to us,
Never we, accountable to you.
Politicians, please, pass it on.

EURO 2020

It's the way they routinely bless themselves,
Those vain and saintly footballers,
Marking themselves with the sign of the Cross
As they take to the field.
And then it's the way they abuse the game,
Seeing not the least contradiction
In their purity of heart,
With routinely committing deliberate fouls—
Crude, injurious, intentional fouls—
In flat contravention of the spirit
And the Rules, of the Beautiful Game.

And it's the way the abuser then denies
What was witnessed, by a million eyes,
Shamelessly raising his innocent hands,
With a face of practised disbelief,
Should the referee even consider
That a foul has been committed.
It's the way they turn sportsmanship inside out,
Able, it seems, to convince themselves
That the End— trophy, pride, wealth, glory—
Entirely justifies these Means.

Nothing, it seems, is troubled,
Inside their professional minds;
Marking themselves with the sign of the Cross
Relieves them of a conscience.
Winning through guile is just as good
As winning through talent and skill.

And thus, corrupted by money and fame,
Is the Corinthian spirit thoroughly quenched,
In the name of the Beautiful Game;
And thus our international sport
Is so piously reduced to nought.

SCHADENFREUDE

In some dank dungeon of my soul,
There squats a warty, clammy presence
My kind and I gave shape and form
Innumerable years ago:
Sired by jealousies perhaps, out of selfishness,
Clinging about my thoughts and feelings,
It seems not possible to avoid
This fat, parasitic toad of Schadenfreude.

When people cheat, and find themselves
Not up the ladder but down the snake,
Or on the inside lane they overtake,
To find they're running out of road,
My sense of their "comeuppance"
Should need no prompting from the toad;
Little incentive to avoid
The clammy touch of Schadenfreude.

But when it's just an accidental thing,
Not of their deserving—
Like a direct hit from a passing bird,
Or your rich friend wears his dinner-jacket,
Well beyond your means,
And spills all down it curried beans—
T'is hardly possible to avoid
The clammy touch of Schadenfreude.

When my closest rival fails a test,
Even as I say, "Bad luck old boy"—
And more so when his partner-to-be
Abandons him and turns to me—
I feel the muffled croak of joy:
How does one possibly avoid,
(Or deny that one is relishing)
This clammy touch of Schadenfreude?

For sometimes, when I'm all alone,
I contemplate this squatting toad,
And think it oddly problematic
To separate its promptings from my own.
Perhaps I'm a little bit not very nice,
Inventing a toad to cover my vice—
And I'm not even sure I want to avoid
This satisfying croak of Schadenfreude.

STEREOTYPES

It may stretch our imaginations—
But let it do so, is my plea:
That from time to time, between
Eighteen thirty-seven, and
Nineteen hundred and one,
Victorian Fathers could be found,
Who loved their children, romped around
With them, gave them piggy-backs, and
Read them bedtime stories.

And let's allow imaginations
Further scope and licence,
Allowing that a scion of our Aristocracy
Could give away State Secrets,
Denying all offences
And fiddling his expenses.

Allowing there are Politicians,
Who simply can't be bought,
Who answer questions candidly
Without a cautious thought
For their own political skins.
Allow for Lawyers who dispense justice,
Irrespective of the law,
Allow that some Slave-Owners,
Dare we say, on occasion
Did show kindness to their slaves;
That there are Vicars who
Do not believe what they are preaching,

Have a flutter on the horses
And give way to dark temptations.
That there are Truckers who follow opera,
Miners who dote on Mozart,
Immigrants who never wish to leave us,
Having never been abused
But always felt so privileged, and welcome.

That there are Army Colonels far from
Pompous, accents as plain as
Mine or yours, whose chief concern
Is the welfare of their soldiers;
That among the Innocents locked in jail,
Some of them probably are—
Outnumbered far by the Guilty,
At liberty and leisure,
Who should be there instead.
A certain elasticity of mind
Is all that we require,
To allow that virtue, taste,
Corruption, shame, and honour,
Are pretty evenly distributed
Through all the social strata.

And then it follows, that if
We are kind and fair to everyone
We meet, all we need do is
Accept people as we find them,
Dumping Stereotypes in the dustbin.

BEST FRIEND

It was only last week, an old friend said
"And this is Colin", indicating his young bulldog—
And today, the lady down the road
Introduced me to her bloodhound bitch,
"Olivia— she's one of the family now".
Both said they were 'walking' them,
And used the very same words:
Not hoping their dogs would defecate,
But would 'go to the toilet'.

Something has been taking place,
While I have been half asleep.
I don't know if it ever was so,
That DOG was chained outside, in his kennel,
As you see in the old cartoons,
But I do remember, in my earlier days,
People's names were kept for people:
Dogs were Woofy, Fido, Rusty, Trixie or Patch—
Our best friends they may have been,
But they jolly well knew their place;
No question of four-legged membership
Of a two-legged human race.
Now, I'm told that people cuddle their dogs,
And kiss their dogs— even sleep beside them.

Has selective breeding come to this?
We wanted a dog to cuddle and kiss?
Far more practical purposes, surely,
Than breeding a biddable kind of canine child,
With a human name to prove it.

Next time I meet young Colin's master,
I've decided to call him Bonzo;
And Olivia's mistress? She shall be Lassie.

LEADING MAN

Heart-warming romances they may be,
Films for all the family,
With, who shall we say, as Leading Man—
Stewart, Brando, Redford, Hanks?
For whom, inevitably, the charming, modest,
Beautiful Leading Lady ultimately falls.

But it's her present young man who touches me,
That buttoned-up bore, approved by her parents;
That bland, characterless loser,
Who touches me more:
I want to call after him, "Don't despair;
Never mind; perhaps in the next film,
Or the one after that..."

I imagine his feelings when 'Casting' calls,
Offering him the part:
"Dress up some swaggering Ego
In fancy pants and shiny shoes,
Give him some swaggering lines to learn,
And any Dope can play the lead.

But supporting parts— not for nothing
Are they called supporting;
Movies would collapse without them—
They call for real talent;
Character-acting, subtle and convincing,
Nuanced, meticulously observed:
Appearing as somebody dumb and lacking,
Calls for somebody very special."

Utterly unconvinced, I dare say,
Suspicious of the compliment,
He sets about learning
The flattest, least-amusing lines,
With all his special talents—
Thankful, in the early scenes at least,
That he will seem to be
The object of her heart's desire—
Before his inevitable eclipse,
Having barely touched the Leading Lady's lips.

I like to think, when he's back at home—
Away from honeyed words, artificial lights,
Away from the set and the script—
He's the most affable, sociable fellow
You could wish to meet;
The friendliest of neighbours—
I want him to be a successful leading man,
Cherished by his loving, homely leading lady—
Fulfilment, tenderness, words hardly needed;
Let him be a wonderful father
To his two young children,
Not by his own estimation— by theirs.

FAVOURITISM

"Were we not as equal sisters nurtured?"
Said starboard sister to her portside twin;
"Never one above the other favoured?"
Said starboard sister to her portside twin—
"Budding, blossoming side by side,
In all coyness, and in quiet pride?
Throughout our schooling, equal marks?
In all examinations tied?
And since bound together the livelong day,
Are we not freed together, by night to play?"

"Why yes, to all," said portside twin;
"Why ask of which you surely know?
What's true for me, is true for you—
Has anyone denied it so?"
"So much prettier, you, than I?"
"Why no!" protested portside twin.
"Less charming, less becoming, than you be?"
"In all particulars, sister, never less than me."
"Less endowed to catch his manly eye?"
"Oh, starboard sister, never less than I!"

"Equally blessed with womanly treasure?
Yet still is portside more his pleasure:
If neither above the other flavoured,
Why port, much more than starboard, savoured?
What sort of blossom is shunned by bees?
Enviable sister, do help me please."

"As impartially as bees to flowers,
So would his lips, these blooms of ours,"
Said portside to her starboard twin,
"But so by nature and by culture trained,
The starboard way, is man constrained:
Salutes, and greets, the starboard way,
And raises thus his glass in toast—
To make a vow, or swear an oath—
By starboard hand, he Plights his Troth:
And so it must be, that a musical fellow,
Always from starboard, as nature taught,
Will tenderly bow his beloved cello,
Instinctively, without a thought—
Cradling his cello, lovingly, to port."

LITTER

So self-evidently preferable,
Is the alternative to dropping litter—
Taking it home for the rubbish-bins,
Leaving our lanes, our hedges and edges
Clear and undefiled, for the pleasure
And the benefit of us all—
That hard-put are we to understand
Why droppers prefer to rubbish our land,
So as to have us characterised
As a nation of careless litterers.

Most of us never need By-laws,
Which express common sense, after all;
We like to think the Laws of a Land
Express the will of its people:
We gladly conform, it follows,
To laws we make for ourselves.
Some explanation there must be,
For what is seldom accidental
But intended, ostentatious even;
Adolescent in the main, it seems,
A simple coming-of-age test
Which too many candidates fail
On purpose, possibly to show
What confident, carefree spirits they are—
A badge of individuality.

Some grow up to join us,
Enhancing our communities,
But far too many drift away
To heavier stuff, sofas, fridges,
'Fly-tippers' in the making.
One wonders how such consciences
Can be wakened from their slumbers.

Meanwhile, let us not mince words:
People who, in public places,
Wantonly scatter their rubbish,
Are thoroughly anti-social,
Amoral, self-indulgent idiots
And— if I may be forgiven—
Are demonstrably 'Illiterate'.

POMPEY

I'm not sure why it matters to me,
But matter to me it does;
Matter to me how Pompey got on
At Fratton Park, or playing away—
Not a lot, I must confess, but
Palpable, perceptible none the less—
Scanning through the League results,
Inevitably looking for theirs.
Fifty years or more since
I was last there, a losing score
Can spoil my evening.

I was not even raised there,
But a Naval acquaintance, in far-off days,
When my ship lay in the harbour there—
In the days of Jimmy Dickenson,
Froggatt, Scoular and Duggie Reed—
In Pompey's patriotic hue,
Red socks, white shorts, shirts of Navy blue.
And even now, in distant times,
Still I hear those Pompey Chimes—
Just as Big Ben tolls the hours,
"Play, Up, Pom, Pey; Pom, Pey, Play, Up".

It should be on our passports, you know,
Alongside names and dates of birth;
Never mind where born or raised—
Which team do you support?
Star-signs defining us, locating us—
And for security purposes:
Mother's maiden name? Football Club?
Equally unlikely to change.

And bless them, they are a Football Club
With a heart and soul: Playing to win
Is such a rusty old concept, unless
You play to win the altruistic, virtue
And morality match, avoiding
Hurting your opponents' feelings
By scoring goals against them:
And think how they must feel,
If you deny them goals against you.

In a Club of such high principles,
Apparent weaknesses over the years,
Unrecognised for what they are,
Have always been tokens of strength.
Come rain or shine, lose, draw or win,
If you are a loyal supporter,
A supporter is what you have to be.

Wonderful thing, this loyalty,
This unconditional loyalty,
Most of a lifetime later,
Even now thumbing a ride
With this, my favourite football side.
And now with these evening bells, I hear,
Summoning me to my rest,
Pompey's unmistakeable chimes—
Loyalty repaid, sounding a truth—
Of all the football teams to follow,
I followed the very best.

THOROUGHBRED

No, it wasn't that photo, of a trainer,
Sitting astride the prostrate body
Of a dead horse, but the response to it—
The official response, from the
Irish Horse Regulatory Board.

An offence against Rule 272, said they;
Prejudicial to the Integrity,
Proper Conduct or
Good Reputation of horse-racing—
Implying, in wording of this sort,
That horse-racing, steeplechasing,
Is self-evidently reputable,
A fine and honourable sport—
And more explicitly, the trainer
Had not shown the 'respect
That an animal in his care
Is entitled to'.
Who knew racehorses were so respected?
Perhaps it's only when they're dead—
Yet when they're dead they have no value;
Perhaps that's it, the value—
Masquerading as respect?

Puzzling ways to show a horse respect:
Deny it any free, wild life;
Keep it captive, a kind of slavery,
Its natural instincts well suppressed
By training and selective breeding;
Neuter any nonsense out;
Make it slavishly obey orders
From its owner, and its rider;
Make it race, and steeplechase.

Hypocrisy, the odds-on Favourite, wins again,
Hypocrisy, trained by Arrogance, ridden by Money,
Leaving Irony, and Parody,
Furlongs in its wake.

STREETWISE

It is by universal franchise,
That governments, in democracies,
Are by majority elected,
And so the laws which they enact,
Not unreasonably, we hope,
Are universally respected.
Nor unreasonable, we hope,
That Police are given powers
Within the law, in public places,
To control and direct the people,
For peace and order on our streets.
Even less unreasonable, we hope,
To oblige the public to accept
And follow their instructions.

And so, one wonders, just what
Do we expect Police Officers to do,
When demonstrators on our streets
Are hostile, truculent,
Defiantly confronting them—
Insulting our law, our government
And our people, the electorate?

If concerted defiance persists,
Only two options, it would seem,
Are available to Police—
To yield our streets to protesters
Or to remove, by legitimate force,
Those abusing our precious freedoms.

If removal is violently resisted,
How can anyone protest
At stronger tactics by the State?
Brutality is not acceptable; suppressing
Mayhem on our streets, surely is.

Policing by consent must mean
Exactly what it promises,
For peace and order in our land:
Just as we insist our Officers
Act within the law,
So we expect and insist that
Grown-up people on our streets
Submit to their instructions.

CUSTOMER

Who would be a customer? How many
Times do Companies begin their letters,
"As a valued customer, we are grateful for …"
Valued? They haven't even the courtesy
To write grammatical English.
Today, I am waiting, and waiting—
It is one of those waiting days:
They said they would deliver today,
Though they couldn't be sure what time,
So I've been waiting in, today,
In my homely Waiting Room, for them
To deliver what weeks ago I paid for,
And what I am waiting in for.

I thought, while I was waiting,
I might as well call the Electric People,
To take advantage of their New Plan—
Especially designed for people like me—
I might like to join the queue, said they;
Unusually high demand, said they;
Recommend you try 'on-line', said they,
As I awaited this delivery.

Yesterday morning I was at the clinic
Half an hour ahead of time, fearing
That if I was late, my appointment
Would be missed. "Sorry to keep
You waiting", he said, calling me in,
Twenty-five minutes after time.
I smiled weakly, knowing I needed him
More than he needed me.

So many times, in the couple of years
Before my late wife died, I took her
To various clinics and hospitals,
Arriving, invariably, ahead of time.
I'm sure I would have remembered,
If ever we'd been seen on time:
The worst was an hour and a quarter late,
Waiting, in the Waiting Room, waiting.

In any place that has a Waiting Room,
I guess we must expect to wait,
But there is waiting, and there is waiting:

In bus or railway terminals, or airports,
We expect to get there early, and wait
For departure times as scheduled—
But be a customer, a client, a patient—
Appointments are approximations.

Thus are customers, clients, patients
Subordinated, to those with whom
They've made appointments, agreements:
Imagine the delivery man waiting outside,
Until we decide to open the door;
Imagine the lawyer, waiting outside
Until we're ready to call him in;
Or the doctor smiling weakly,
After waiting so patiently, knowing
She needed me more than I needed her.

It's all a matter status and rank.
We value our customers, but
Once we have banked their money,
They can wait three weeks for delivery—
A matter of status, rank, equality,
Where some are more equal than others.

SUSCEPTIBILITY

In vain I peruse the Dental aisle
In the local supermarket— maybe
Ten or a dozen toothpastes on sale—
No doubt any would clean my teeth
Perfectly well, but none will do:
I'll look elsewhere for that brand
I'm used to, continuously, ever since
I first grew teeth.

Nor, from the Medicines aisle,
Any but that tonic Mother gave us
Before we went to school—
Nor any disinfectant down our drains
But that whose name and fragrance
Evoke the Family Home;
As a tree is trained, so will it grow.

Nor would I trade, for any price,
Loyalty to our football team
Through all its narrow wins and losses,
Since first I kicked a ball.
As a tree is trained, so will it grow.

Early preferences, tastes and smells,
Certain friends of infancy, rituals,
Colours, even the names of things,
Are apt to remain, like some
Resistant dye or stain,
Unmoved by growing up,
Imprinted, indelible —
Susceptibilities in our early years,
Long perceived and understood
By Elders in Religious Orders.

ECKS

Of all our six-and-twenty letters,
I wonder what the twenty-fourth has done,
To curry favour with, or bribe us all:
It is no easier to voice, than others;
A little easier to write, I suppose,
Than most, one stroke crossing out the other.

Yet it seems to have stepped forward
From the ranks, and volunteered, while
More modest letters stood there, watching:
It seems to have a quality of boldness—
One volunteer is worth two pressed men, I know—
But is there, I ask myself,
Some ignoble, ulterior motive?

For upper case or lower case,
It's always keen to show its face—
Versatility, or arrogance? I'm not so sure:
At elections, when we go to Vote,
Do we indicate our preference with a V?
Oh no; the ubiquitous X it has to be.
And oh, doesn't it love to wrap itself
In mystery! 'x', the unknown quantity—
Infiltrating algebra the whole world over—
Find me if you can, but first,
Problems and equations must be solved.

Romans used it as Number Ten, I know,
But it was a fairly junior number—
Senior to I and to V, I grant you—
But heavily outranked by L, C, D and M,
So that's not much to shout about.

I bet it doesn't feel so cocky
When Homework's being marked,
For when the Teacher puts an X,
It means you've got it wrong!
And that horizontal axis
Is nothing to write home about—
Still less on that Certificate
On films we weren't allowed to see.

See how it flatters us, whenever it can:
Three X's on a bottle of ale, is better
Than two, better for a masculine man like you,
In your jackets and trousers of XXXL.

Its bloated self-importance knows no limit—
The basic building-blocks of life, no less:
It sticks itself on Chromosomes—
Two for every woman, one for every man,
In such a showy, chivalrous manner—
Constantly currying favour.

How on Earth did it come to denote
A kiss? My hunch is, we can all
See though its desperate ruses:
It can have only minimal, supporting roles
In forming words, and so it tries to
Put itself about, and seem important—
Apparently unashamed to be on Birthday Cards,
And Xmas Cards, representing kisses—
Or could this have been its scheming,
Underlying purpose, all along?

GULLWAY BAY

On the way to our isolated holiday cottage,
Overlooking Galway Bay,
Our taxi turned into a bleak estate
Of modern-looking houses.
We exchanged forlorn glances,
And then we recognised, from the photo
In the paper, the house where the
Taxi stopped; and then that feeling,
That exquisitely embarrassing feeling,
Of having been duped, defrauded,
Deceived, taken-in, made fools of.

The photo in the paper was a close-up;
Exclusive, so as to fill the frame,
As might suggest a solitary place.
Instead of wondering what lay to the left,
The right, and behind the camera,
We naively took it at its word.
When later we trudged to the edge
Of the estate, we needed our binoculars
For any close appreciation
Of the wonderful Galway Bay.
"Quarter of a mile from a thatched pub",
The advertisement said.
So that was the shameful evocation:
A cottage in rustic isolation,
Overlooking Galway Bay,
With an old, thatched country pub
To welcome you, just along the lane.

The pub in the estate was indeed thatched,
But with all the rustic ambience
Of a dentist's waiting-room.

Such heartless advertisers,
With consciences evidently clear,
Will avoid explicitly saying
What is patently untrue—

But routinely they will imply,
Lead us to infer,
And by omission falsify—

Taking our money without a qualm,
With so little respect for us—
Breeding only cynicism, forever,
Among families browsing through the Ads.

HELPER

The boy was about four, I guess,
When he hurried out to help his Dad,
Who was cleaning the family car.
Copying his Dad, taking a sponge
From a bucket, sploshed muddy water:—
That lovely young fellow had muddied
What his Dad had just been cleaning.
His father failed; why, I can only guess,
And 'tutted' in exasperation—
Such that that admirable lad, who'd come
To help his Dad, hurried back inside,
In some distress.

There's a chance he may not remember,
For he was no more than four;
But that moment will live with me,
His Dad, for evermore.

KNEE-TAKING

Have I not 'Taken the Knee'?
No, I have not 'Taken the Knee'—
Less Holy than thou, must I be.
How can people know I care,
Without my striking silly poses?
Clearly, we who do not 'Take the Knee'
Are xenophobic, racist bigots,
Lost for all Eternity.

It seems entirely fitting,
That you wait for the Referee's whistle,
Before collectively 'Taking the Knee',
And wait for the following whistle
Before you hand it back,
Standing upright on your feet—
A solemn, public demonstration
Of ostentatious mindlessness:
One wonders how many toots of the whistle;
One wonders how many cracks
Of the Ringmaster's whip it will take,
To make you think for yourselves.

Just what are you trying to tell us,
All you who solemnly 'Take the Knee'?
That what's the point of virtue
If we do not advertise it?
Virtue dwells within itself,
It needs no flags nor banners.

It's the advertising of yourselves,
With all its implication
That we who do not 'Take the Knee'
Are thus less honourable than thee,
That so much tries the patience
Of we who think for ourselves.

CHILD'S EYES

As soon as the child was able
To sit up to the breakfast table,
And learn to spoon for herself,
She pointed to the pattern on the cereal bowl,
With evident surprise and joy,
As if to point it out to me—
Sprays of celandine and cranesbill,
Delicately crafted in yellows and blues.

Several thousand times had I washed
And dried those cereal bowls,
With what indifferent and distracted eyes—
Celandines and cranesbill quite unseen—
Since I bought that set, years before;
But there was little in that child's mind
To intervene, between the child
And what the child's eyes had seen.

What a world of simple joy
We hasten past, quite unsighted
By duties and routines:
We seem to know it, in motifs, designs,
Tributes to the natural, in the Arts.
That world of simple joy awaits us,
As soon as we prioritise,
And see, once again, through child's eyes.

ONE TO TEN

Obediently, eternally, we orbit,
Captivated by our Sun:
Twelve months on, finding ourselves
Where the previous orbit had begun,
We reckon that One Year—
And give each year a number,
On a system based on One to Ten,
One to a Hundred, One to a Thousand
For, as we have been taught,
There never was a 'Year Nought'.

The end of one hundred years,
The turn of a century,
Seems to call for a celebration,
And our forebears seem to have known
That there can be no Hundred Years,
Even though three digits change,
Until you've counted in the Hundredth.
Thomas Hardy's poignant piece,
'The Darkling Thrush', when
Nineteenth became the Twentieth Century,
Is dated Thirty-first December,
In the year Nineteen Hundred,
Observing that the Twentieth Century
Began in Nineteen Hundred and One.

If a turn of a hundred years
Calls for celebrations,
How much more the turn of a thousand,

When not only fourth, third and second,
But all four digits change,
Heralding a New Millenium?

But it was just this numerical switch
That had the power to bewitch:
To change a world of 'One-to-Tenners'
Into mindless 'Nought-to-Niners',
Planning a global jamboree,
One full year before it was due.
Being a pedantic sort of chap,
I forewarned our Home Office,
As I trust many others did,
Hoping to spare the Nation's blushes,
And perhaps the entire world's.

In a rather sheepish reply,
They, sort of conceded the point,
Suggesting that the year Two Thousand
Might be regarded as an extended
New Century's Eve, Millenium's Eve,
Until Two Thousand and One began:
And so it was, that appearances,
A dazzling change of numbers,
Triumphed over tedious facts.

With most of a thousand years to go,
Before the next Millenium turn—
If we continue to orbit the Sun,
There should be ample time to prepare
For the dawn of Three Thousand and One.

"ISMS"

A plague of blind self-righteousness
Has brought us all out in a
Rash, an itchy rash of 'isms':
If you are a 'white' person, blemishes
Will show more clearly on your skin,
For Racism is inborn;
If you are a 'white' male person,
Likely there'll be ulcers as well,
For Sexism is ingrained;
If you are 'white', male and elderly,
Your pustules have begun to reek—
Ageism simply poisons souls;
And for such a fellow loving his country,
No therapy is known to man—
Patriotism— moribund, execrable.

For such a blind, self-righteous plague,
Satire seems the only hope,
For none so blind as will not see,
Whose blindness never is of sight,
But chronic blindness in the mind—
And never let it be supposed,
Any fault resides in those
Who brandish sanctimonious 'isms'.

It must be we, the poor possessed,
Wretched, cursed by very birth,
Who must for our salvation sue,
And beg what penance may be due,
To purge and banish loathsome 'isms'
With disinfecting exorcisms.

Though there might be just a chance
That some purveyors of this plague
May find arousal from their trance,
Awaken from their blinkered sleep—
Visit their flushing toilet,
Then water, hot and cold, on tap,
With public utilities, electric or gas—
Cook a breakfast for themselves,
Listening to the broadcast views
Of Home and International News—
Peruse a newspaper of their choice,
Of several in our open press
Allowing freedom of expression,
Where they may read about our welfare state,
Our regular elections, secret ballots,
Freedoms of travel and assembly,
Our long-established legal system,
Proceedings open to the public.

So many benefits are ours,
That idiots have to cast around—
For something to be indignant about:
There might be just a chance,
That purveyors of this silly plague
Will actually ponder, as they sip
Their morning coffee, butter their toast,
That overshadowing their peevish 'isms'
There breathes a country better than most,
And probably many foreign nations
More worthy of their protestations.

TOKYO OLYMPICS

Finals, in major sporting tournaments,
As a general rule are much less exciting
Than Semi-Finals, and the reason seems to be
So much anticipation, speculation, 'build-up'
To a bubble of expectation that
Can only burst, on Finals Day,
Guaranteeing anti-climax.

After qualifying events, every four years,
Olympic Games fall prey to
Just such relentless speculation,
From just such broadcast preliminaries.
And it's not so much in take-your-turn events,
But in the Races, the simultaneous
Encounters, that Commentators spoil the show,
By falling prey themselves.
Funny old things, these Races, people
Running or swimming, or riding
Together as fast as they can, trying
To reach the end before anyone else:
One wonders why it should matter—
Who comes first, or second, and so on.

We encourage it to matter, sure enough,
With medals, reputations, kudos
All at stake, whereto the athletes
Train for years and years,
So that witnessing Olympic Races
Is intrinsically thrilling—

'Intrinsic', 'inherited', may be the very words
For a deep survival instinct, premium
Placed on speed, in catching prey
Or avoiding being caught.

For it does seem likely, that Commentators
Subliminally enact our primitive thrills,
So incontinent are their words and images—
Likening a swimmer to Neptune, Poseidon,
Declaring performances stratospheric,
Heaven for some, Hell for others, no less;
Not merely 'Glory' versus 'Heartbreak',
But Heaven for a medal, Hell for anything less.

And if we need Commentators at all,
Let them explain, set the scene, by all means,
Identify competitors for us—
No need describe what we're watching
For ourselves, no need for frantic
Shredding of their vocal cords to
Dramatise the whole thing for us:
If the Race is thrilling, we will
Be thrilled, in our own individual ways;
If it isn't, we will not be.

From all of which should follow, something more—
A dignity, restraint, in victory:
Medals were not 'up for grabs',
As Commentators told us,
But rewards for sporting excellence,
Within a true Olympic ethos.
Now that you've proved you're the fastest,
A gold standard let there be
In your modesty, nobility of manner.
Let there be containment in celebration:
Just as there is no tragedy, nor disgrace
In losing, neither is it a war
You've won, simply a Sport, a Game.
To tear off your shirt, aggressively
Punch the air, writhe on the ground,
Performing for the cameras,
Is to lose all sight of the purposes
Underlying Sports, and Games—

Such as developing health, well-being;
Releasing pent-up energies and
Inhibitions, giving vent to
Wilder feelings, deepening self-confidence;
Bridging gaps between peoples, cultures—
To lose sight of all this,
Focussing on the medals, the podium,
Sanctifying above all, Rank Order,
Even, may Heaven Forbid,
Creating Damehoods and Knighthoods,
Is to miss, by a sorry Country Mile,
The purposes of Sports and Games.

HONOURS

In weighing up worthiness for Honours,
They consider whether those proposed
"Made life better for other people", or
"Are outstanding at what they do".
Not 'and', mark you, but 'or'— If you
Are outstanding at anything— be it
Entirely self-serving, with no pretence
Of enhancing other people's lives—
You can be considered for the Honours Lists.
Thus we read our sportswriters,
Appearing to incline and prompt
Her Majesty the Queen, no less,
To bestowing her Damehoods,
And bestowing her Knighthoods,
Upon athletes from Olympic Games.

Honours are intended for those who
"Made achievements in public life", who
"Committed themselves to serving and
Helping Britain". Public, surely,
Only in that their achievements
Are publicly witnessed.
And are we to infer their overriding purpose
Was in serving and helping Britain?
My guess is that any profit to their country,
By way of national prestige, or reputation,
Is entirely incidental, that no such grandiose,
Altruistic, selfless thoughts entered
Their young minds, when they first
Showed such promising talent.

Even if, competing in your sport,
You are conspicuously noble, good-
Hearted and fair-minded, it merely
Shows that those amongst whom you
Are distinguished, are less so—
And that you clearly understand
What your sport demands of you.
And even if, giving your very best,
You do not win— it is no failure
When you smile with dignity, and good grace:
You have not lost but won, in sporting terms,
A sporting gold, personified.

How much more then, are we entitled
To expect, from winners, just pride
And satisfaction with their medals,
Their fame and adulation.

No more should we expect our
Ancient House of Lords to be
Peopled by civil servants 'honoured'
For simply serving their time,
Than the Dames and Knights of
Our ancient land be chosen
By how fast they could run,
Or how high they could jump.

If an Olympic gold medal, or two,
Or three, is not sufficient reward
For you, then you are something
Less than sporting: You simply fail
To understand the purpose of your sport.

NEIGHBOURS

It is no surprise, but noticeable
Nonetheless, that things are going
Well for me this week, as I
Tick off appointments in my Diary,
Nor any surprise that it's the people
I meet, who make it so:
How lucky, to live in a country
Where smiles and helpfulness are not exceptions
But the daily, general rule.

The 'lads' at the garage are every bit
As obliging as they are efficient
And thorough in what they do. There was
A courtesy car for me to drive—
But when it's not available, they
Drive me two miles home, and bring
My car back when the job is done.

The dentist was her usual reassuring
Self, explaining everything she did,
Praising me for my dental care, and
Pleased that I had lost some weight.
All very much the same
As in the doctors' surgery:
Reception and Dispensary staff
Unfailingly courteous, driven by
What they can do to help —
GP's, male and female, no less so.

And so, with the friendly builders,
Who keep my cottage in good repair—
As dependable as they are thorough,
With such pride in their work,
And that affable good humour.

When I pop in to the Village Stores
For my Saturday papers, the owner
Always has them ready, always
With welcoming, neighbourly words,
Good-nature personified.

Nor have Supermarkets in Ross
Entirely lost the personal touch
Of independent High-Street shops:
However tedious, stacking shelves
Or operating checkouts,
There is such friendly chat and banter.

When I got home, with my groceries,
There, in the porch, was a bag
Of garden-fresh veg— onion,
Kale and runner-beans, left there
By the kind of neighbours who
Enrich neighbourhoods, quite as
Nourishing to any community
As any garden-fresh veg could be.

As is my wont, while unpacking,
I turned on Radio Four: It was
Woman's Hour tutorial time, further
Studies from their Curriculum
Of Umbrage, laying bare the
Sordid facts of English Life:
Once more, I learned of brutalised
Womanhood, relentless degradation
Of womankind in a patriarchy
Of arrogant, toxic masculinity.

SOUND EFFECTS

The origin of everything that is, or was,
Or will be, so defies explaining
That Science reaches for Philosophy,
Theology apparently abstaining.
Back through immeasurable Time,
Something, somehow led to us,
And a cataclysmic detonation
Is the leading scientific guess:
If anything is the ultimate focal point
For man's faculty of awe
And wonder, it is this.

But in the hands of our BBC—
Part of our earthly speck in the vastness—
This faculty cannot be left
To its own devices— to speculate
In silence, thrilling, personal silence:

No dramatic reconstruction
Of our supposed cosmic origins
Can be left to our thoughts;
Directed and prescribed
Must our responses be,
By humanoid soaring orchestras,
And humanoid celestial choirs.

It is much the same on the
Natural History front— the wilderness
Teems with immemorial sounds—
Comforting haunting, comical,
Exhilarating, terrifying, mesmerising—
But there's nothing in our natural world,
Making our senses tingle, that our BBC
Will not irritatingly, patronisingly
Intercept and package for us:
That which we wish to listen to,
Drowned out by that we do not.
Of being assumed a retarded half-wit,
I am heartily sick and tired.
Is there any hope of our beloved BBC
Listening to the British Public,
If it will not listen to me?

PROPRIETY

There can be nothing more natural,
Nothing more commonplace and central,
Nothing less surprising than
The coming together of female and male,
For the purpose of procreating.

But insofar as the female and the male
Are human, self-consciously human,
An unforeseen predicament, Morality,
Stands in our way, for the encounter
Serves an extra purpose now—
Not only instinctive now—
But imagined and much adapted,
Not only for producing babies,
But for such incidental pleasure.
And herein seems to lie
A public wondering, debating,
For along comes civilisation,
With all its standards and conventions,
Incorporating sexual matters.
To what extent private and personal?
To what extent of public interest?
Beneath the ebbs and flows of public taste,
And tides of 'acceptable' exposure,
Undercurrents will always tug—
Always challenging standards.
Law-makers dabbling in Morality,
Face an uncomfortable, shifting task,
Presuming to determine public taste,
In the name of the nation's moral health.

In my lifetime, so far, the trend
Has been, increasingly, to make public
What perhaps was best left private—
Most noticeably revealed in Cinema.
In early years, I can recall,
If films touched on the matter at all,
The couple would close the bedroom door,
The camera discreetly left outside;
'Somewhat suggestive', people would say.

These days, we not only watch them
Undressing, in such an inviting way,
But the camera follows them into bed:
Precious, intimate moments, in private—
Private moments for the world to watch—

Little, by way of forwarding the story,
Rather, as pornographic trimmings.

At once embarrassed and engrossed,
Most of us will watch, with all
Degrees of disapproval, and interest.

But tides of public taste do turn,
And the line between tender
Expressions of love, and rank
Obscenity is misty, and negotiable;
Let us hope to stay on the lighter,
Softer side of this precious, defining line.

STANDING STONES

Our Neolithic ancestors, long before
We had languages, to write and read,
Knew that they were children of Sun;
Unquestionably knew, that nothing grew
But for the shining light of Sun—
Grasses, leaves and roots,
Animal flesh, and fruits—
All, all, the progeny of Sun.

They left behind them, Standing Stones—
In henges, lines and circles:
Stones reclining, evidently would not do,
So at huge expense of ingenuity and labour,
Vast Stones must be erected,
In patterns, so as to pay
Tribute, where tribute must be due,
To Sun, comforting, benevolent light,
Acknowledging the summer Solstice,
Casting shadows of obeisance, the whole year round.
What a depressing irony, then:
Later Christian missionaries,
With all their credulous fervour,
Preaching the Gospel of the One True God
To primitive, benighted tribes,
Scorning, demeaning their ancestral rites—
Spirits of the forest, and the waters,
Nature personified, in wondrous dread—

Preaching instead, the Tallest of Tales,
Preaching to those hapless peoples
Not the Natural, but the Supernatural—
Not the Sun, but God in Heaven.
Not magic, though it would seem to be,
But as it is the Gospel Truth,
Believe it you must; have Faith.

Why else, at huge expense and labour,
Would we design, erect Cathedrals,
Basilicas, Temples of Stone,
Vast, proud, Standing Structures—
With towers and vaults and steeples,
With many a worshipful window
Acknowledging the light of the Sun —
  Casting shadows of obeisance, the whole year round.

HISTORY LESSON

It seems as if it's perfectly clear:
Never has there been territorial strife,
Never a hint of tribal tensions;
Unheard of, racial persecution,
No Jim Crow Laws, no colonial wars;
No apartheid, no race riots,
Pogroms, ethnic cleansing, genocide—
From the beginning, right up to now.

For, if there had been,
What sober, grown-up woman or man
Would steer towards these treacherous rocks,
Seduced, unminded by the Siren's Call
For relentless multiculturalism?
"Diversity," she sings, "Diversity is all:
Mingling of cultures, mixing of races,
Enriching, open immigration"—
Blowing us all a promising kiss
For a world of multicultural bliss.

Can you imagine, if this creed persists—
This creed that will hear nor truth nor sense—
What awaits us on those treacherous rocks
A couple of centuries hence?
Neither can I, and I dare not try:
Whom the gods wish to destroy, they first make mad:
Of all the graven images, of all
The false gods we've ever worshipped,
This must be the maddest,
From the beginning, right up to now.

As various and precious as cultures are—
By native land and way of life so rooted—
To be cherished, preserved, not diluted.
A hearty Yes to foreign travel and adventures;
Exchanges educational and sporting.
But surely No to overflowing boundaries—
Less of 'breaking down barriers',
More of shaking hands across them.
Within hospitable cultures,
Immigration trickle can make sense,
Hostess and guest mutually blest.
But Numbers are of the essence,
And incoming cultures, uncontrolled,
Spreading, chafing against the old,
Grow not so much welcomed, as tolerated—
Divided loyalties, territorial wedge—
And people daring not to speak their minds,
From the beginning, right up to now.

Let's not hide from History, but profit from it;
Not test tolerance until it snaps,
But have the courage to place a limit;
Wax our ears to the Siren's Song—
To save our native ways of life,
Each culture loyal to its own.

DEVELOPMENT

Please think twice before you return
To where you were raised,
And played as a child;
Very likely, you will be saddened.

For there are houses there now,
Where you played, houses and
Concrete paths, a housing estate
Where you played, near where
The farmer's livestock grazed.

In the euphemistic jargon of the Planners,
This is called 'Development':
Your area, your fields and trees
Have not been destroyed,
They have been 'Developed',
And so have greenswards, hedges,
Ponds, scrubland and trees
Up and down our land.
We can all see it happening— but
Evidently powerless to resist.
Incalculable losses to our native land
Yet someone, no doubt, somewhere
No doubt, profits from all of this.

If it should prove they grub up fields,
If it should prove they fell the trees,
To make more space for houses;
If it should prove they need the houses
To house a growing population;
And if a growing population
Is largely due to immigration,
It hardly takes a Nobel Prize
To open up the nation's eyes.

Simple Simon, who met the pieman,
Offers a Simple Remedy:
To those who wish to emigrate,
Bid them Bon Voyage;
To those who wish to immigrate,
They will simply have to wait.

But lives there, breathes there, dares there
A politician, to take up Simon's remedy?
It is in the saving of political skins,
That their moral cowardice begins.
Full well they know, latter-day Simons
Are not so simple; full well
They know what happens to them.

At the mercy, then, we fall
Of Developers, whose blandishments
Know no bounds, painting
Planned Developments in quaint, idyllic hues—
Squire's Meadow, Hollybush Close, The Oaks,
Hawthorn Grove and Willow Walk—
As if they sense we are beguiled,
As chocolate ice-cream to a child.
And what of St. Mary's Garden Village,
Supplanting peaceful fields near here?
Think not of soulless rows of houses,
But think a Village, an instant Village,
And a Garden Village at that,
With all its rustic evocations,
Blessed by the Holy Mother Herself.

So spare yourself, please, that sadness;
Keep unblemished, early times,
As recollections in your mind,
Carefree under summer skies.

But dedicate yourself to the Counter Cause
Of the people's voices being heard:
No more usurping of democracy;
Democracy is bottom-to-top,
Or it is nothing but dictatorship
Dressed up in all its arrogance.

To enjoy universal franchise,
By secret ballot, regular elections,
Would suggest that, ultimately,
The electorate's voice is sovereign—
Then make it clear to those we elect:

No more bulldozing of our Heritage,
No more growth of population.
'Development' stops right Here and Now,
Immigration stops right Here and Now;
Insist that politicians, Here and Now,
Listen to the electorate, Here and Now;
But don't just listen to us—
For Heaven's sake, stop 'Developing'
This, our native land.

DELIVERANCE

There is no understanding of that
Which craves to be understood—
Ever since that evolutionary cuckoo
Deposited her fateful egg—
Leaving us to scratch our way
Out of benign and blissful ignorance,
Out into all of this.
No understanding of quite why—
For all our opposable thumbs, cranial space,
Inventiveness and thoughts;
For all our standing tall, assuming command,
Focussing the Earth upon ourselves—
We seemed to need a purpose,
And had no purpose but our own:
We needed point, in pointlessness.

So from our thoughts we wove a comfort,
Drew it over heads and minds
As destiny, purpose, refuge,
From all of this out here—
As if we had been chosen,
Exalted and cocooned,
Awaiting sweet and just Deliverance.

CONUNDRUM

There may be truths we will never know,
Because we stand too close to them—
And one of these would seem to be
The coincidence of body and soul:
And this would challenge the orthodox,
The wisdom of the ages —
That our souls, our feelings and desires,
Are quite distinct from flesh and blood,
Existing independently, from which
It follows, that when the mortal flesh expires,
Immaterial souls endure.

It is my guess, but more than a guess—
I simply cannot help but feel—
The two relate as aliases, body and soul,
The one, proof and evidence of the other;
Manifesting in separate states, rather as
Ice melts, vapour condenses, being both water;
The one expressive of the other,
As trembling will express our fears,
Or consequent to its alter-ego,
Distress be rendered into tears.

What possible emanations, then,
Are these I'm wary of, to save
My reputation, when I'm gone?
For death seems unequivocal,
Oblivious, insensate, gone—
Along with all the consequential senses.

How to reconcile this, then,
With wondering what they'll think of me,
When they no longer need be polite,
Sorting through my 'things', throughout the house;
It seems to matter, what they will think,
My admirable son and daughter:
Preposterous contradiction, knowing I'll be well
Past caring, but caring what they will think.

RESTLESS APPARITION

More and more, it is reported,
An Apparition can be seen—
An Apparition of that great man
Who delivered us all from Evil;
From people far and wide, forever in his debt,
More and more it is reported—
Restlessly pacing the cliffs of Dover,
With a scowl on its resolute features—
Or haunting our beaches, our fields, streets, hills,
Muttering, muttering over and over.

"What was wrong, for Heaven's sake,
With our British words for British measures—
Inch, foot, yard, mile— our birthright,
In native, plain, single syllables
Inherited down the centuries?
That we must choke our British throats
With indigestible polysyllables—
Millimetres, centimetres, metres, kilometres—
Metres! Metres! Blasted Metres!
For Heaven's sake, what was wrong
With inches, feet, yards and miles,
With stones and pounds and ounces,
Gallons and acres and fathoms—
Could it be, that they were British?"

Now and again, it's said, the Apparition pauses,
And turns to face inland,
Draws on a phantom Havana, raises
It's hand in a Victory Sign,
With a sad, incredulous cry—
"They did not need a Trojan Horse;
Some pagan, infidel, philistine within,
Some iconoclastic Traitor,
Harnessed a horse of his own, urging it
Ride roughshod over our language,
Defecating dollops of alien words—
About as tasty on the British tongue
As lumpy, steaming, horsey dung!
Such, from an enemy, hateful curse;
But, from our own politicians?
So, so, so much worse.

The slumbering Hercules, within us,
Must rouse, must and will rouse, I say,
One Victorious, British Day,
Purging the stinking, metric stables
With all our refreshing, British rivers,
And homely, colloquial English words—
Allowing me to rest in peace."

SWEET REAPER

Sweet Reaper, be my guest;
It's Harvest Time; it's time for rest.
Come right in, Old Friend,
I've been expecting you.

This life, it never was my own,
Just trusted to me,
Some bewildering kind of loan—
Now, what was borrowed
Is what I owe,
And now it's time for me to go,
Sweet Reaper, be my guest;
It's time, Old Friend, to pay my dues.

But, if you please, excuse
The very best of me, that stays,
Outlives my days—
More than a name on a family tree,
Things I'd wish the world to see,
Rescuing my thoughts, ideas;
Things I've made, or saved, or written down;
Lessons learned to pass along,
Songs with wings for coming years—

Moving over in some style,
Now that it's time to take my rest,
Hoping it was all worthwhile:
Come, Sweet Reaper, be my guest.

BURIAL

No, not cremation, thank you; have a heart:
As unhurriedly as I was composed,
So leisurely be my ending —
Not a blaze up a brick-lined chimney,
And a scattering of my bits.
No, just a quiet burial please:
Being 'laid to rest'
Sounds about right for me;
I wish to bear more witness
To my dissolving, than I did
To my formation— befriend my end.
I've pondered it, my whole life through,
My death, as metamorphosis.

What's the great hurry anyway?
We slower-witted ones, you know,
Couldn't crash and trample through the world—
We had to pause, to look around,
Reflect on things, take it all in;
Just so, insist on savouring decline.
We had to wait nine months or so
Simply to open our eyes;

Some such leeway then, at the end,
In the drift of our own demise.

The final time a curtain falls,
Dramatis Personae disperse,
Resigned to playing different parts,
And my living, as my dying, wish
Is to follow my Natural History through,
Enriching the soil in deep repose,
Subconscious, as I decompose—
I hardly know just what I mean,
But the soil belongs to me
As much as I belong to the soil—
And the soil, ah, this soil:
Nothing will do but English soil,
And English soil is feet and inches:
Six feet six will do just fine.

And in this peaceful English trench,
Think you not of any stench
But of captivating fragrance,
As if to serve a purpose—
Of course, to serve a purpose—
Nature making perfect sense,
Pure, innate benevolence,
Recycling and reviving,
With all her husbandry and thrift.

If you should ever be in doubt
Of her everlasting providence,
You'll find it writ in the underground press:
Look in the weekly Microbial Times,
Under 'Burials ... Forthcoming Events':
'Eight-Week Aromatic Banquet—
Book Early— Only Two Trillion Places'.

Author Biography

Robert Choulerton was born in 1937 in Rawalpindi, India (now Pakistan), to Joe, a soldier serving with the British Army, and his wife Violet. When the family returned to England, Robert was all of six months old.

He started school in Rhyl, where the family was based during the War. When Joe was demobilised in 1946, the family moved to Wiltshire. Robert attended Corsham Council School, and Chippenham Grammar School.

In 1953, he joined the Royal Navy as an Artificer Apprentice – serving for 24 years. In 1961 he was commissioned, after training at Britannia Royal Naval College, Dartmouth. He served in a Mine-Hunter flotilla in UK and Scandinavian waters, an Aircraft-Carrier in the Far East and a Frigate on the West Indies station. In 1969, he trained for the Submarine Service, and on promotion served in two Polaris nuclear submarines, running deterrent patrols.

During his service, he read for a BA (Hons) degree with the Open University. He retired from the Royal Navy in 1977, in the rank of Lieutenant Commander.

After a Postgraduate Certificate in Education at Bath University, he taught English at Wellsway Comprehensive School, Keynsham. In 1984–5 he took secondment to read for an MA at the University of Exeter.

Taking early retirement in 1990, he worked as Secretary of Lansdown Tennis and Squash Club, Bath.

He now lives in Lea Bailey, near Ross-on-Wye. His late wife died in 2013. He has a son and daughter from a previous marriage, and four grandchildren.

www.ingramcontent.com/pod-product-compliance
Lightning Source LLC
LaVergne TN
LVHW041332080426
835512LV00006B/417